THE
BOOK
OF
NUMBERS

Also by William Hartston

The Psychology of Chess (with Peter Wason)
The Ultimate Irrelevant Encyclopaedia (with Jill Dawson)
Chess: The Making of the Musical
The Drunken Goldfish
How Was It For You, Professor?
Short v Kasparov, 1993
Teach Yourself Chess
Teach Yourself Better Chess
The Guinness Book of Chess Grandmasters

THE
BOOK
OF
NUMBERS

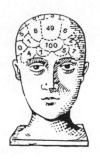

WILLIAM
HARTSTON

RICHARD COHEN BOOKS London

British Library Cataloguing in Publication Data:
A catalogue for this book is available from the British Library

Copyright © 1997 by William Hartston

ISBN 1 86066112 2

First published in Great Britain in 1997 by
Richard Cohen Books
7 Manchester Square
London W1M 5RE

The right of William Hartston to be identified as
the author of this work has been asserted by him in
accordance with the Copyright, Designs and
Patents Act 1988

Design by Craig Dodd

Typeset in Gill Sans and Garamond by
MATS, Southend-on-Sea, Essex

Printed in Great Britain by
T.J. Press International
Padstow, Cornwall

CONTENTS

Preface

This is a book about numbers – to be more exact, the positive integers from one to 4,985,567,071,200. The journey stops at all stations until we reach the boiling point of water on the Fahrenheit scale, then proceeds at an ever-increasing rate towards its destination. This is not, primarily, a history of numbers or of counting, though anyone interested in those topics will find a good deal of relevant material in the pages that follow. It is not about the mathematical theory of numbers, though many arithmetical curiosities will be found here also. Neither is this just a compilation of number-related lists, though you will find many of those here too. There is also plenty of information about numbers in films, numbers in literature, numbers in song, numbers in nature, indeed, numbers wherever you might encounter them.

This is, in short, a book of numbers unlike any other book of numbers. What I have tried to do is assemble a collection of number-related information and arrange it in numerical order. As a work of reference, it is designed to answer any question beginning with the words 'How many . . . ?', particularly questions that you would never have thought of asking in the first place.

You will find some information on every number from 1 to 212, after which the entries become more sporadic. I have included an introduction to each of the numbers from 1 to 100, to give a guide to the character of the number and particular facts or superstitions that may be related to it. After 100, with a few, too important to overlook, exceptions, you are generally left on your own to draw whatever conclusions you choose from the facts supplied.

I have resisted the temptation to give systematic coverage to any particular sphere, preferring simply to collect and collate information as I bumped into it, or it into me. This accounts for the totally unsystematic policy regarding units of measurement. You will find miles jostling alongside kilometres, pounds next to kilograms, Celsius on equal footing with Fahrenheit. My only rule has been to keep all measurements in the same units as I first encountered them.

You may open the book wherever you like and start reading. Indeed, the material may perhaps be best enjoyed in the same manner in which it has been collected: totally haphazardly. The only signposts are an occasional → which I have inserted to point towards a related entry under another number.

Acknowledgements

I should like to thank all of my friends and colleagues who have helped my researches by supplying me with their cast-off numbers. The reference works I have consulted are too numerous to mention, but I owe a particular debt of gratitude to the various encyclopaedias on CD-ROM that make the search for numerical information so much easier than it once was. There is a brief bibliography of the works I found most useful, and which the reader in search of more information might consult.

■ Zero

There were no people injured by tea-cosies in Britain in 1994 (though three had been treated in hospital in the previous year as a result of tea-cosy accidents).

Zero is also the number of times the word 'Bible' occurs in the works of Shakespeare.

Those items, however, do not really concern us. For this book is about the positive integers, from 1 to almost five trillion.

■ I

'One is one and all alone and ever more shall be so.'
From *The Dilly Song*, also known as *Green Grow the Rushes-O*

The ancient Greeks did not consider one to be a number at all. Euclid had defined 'number' as an 'aggregate of units', so one is not so much a number itself as the mother of all numbers. Even more oddly, however, they regarded the number one as both odd and even – perhaps simply to support its unique (from the Latin, *unus*; one) claim to be both male and female and thus the number from which all others sprang.

In religious mysticism, one represents God, while in numerology one is associated with the Sun, and with everything positive and original. Linguistically, one-ness is signified by the prefixes mono- or uni- (including the words unity, union and universe), while even the words 'a', 'an' and 'alone' are etymologically close relatives of 'one'.

One is also the number of:
Butler schools in the US
cases of acute poliomyelitis in the UK in 1995
centimetres of hair grown each month
dead heats in the Oxford-Cambridge boat race
elephants in Alaska in 1995 (the date when the Alaskans changed their
    laws relating to the keeping of elephants specifically to allow one
    ex-circus elephant to stay there)
eyes on a Cyclops
heliports in Algeria
hiccups in the works of Shakespeare (uttered, appropriately enough, by
    Sir Toby Belch in *Twelfth Night*)

3 Men in a boat (Jerome K Jerome)

horns on a unicorn

minutes each year the average Haitian spends making international
    phone calls

paintings sold by Vincent van Gogh in his lifetime

public telephones in Kabul

recorded accidents in the home in the UK in 1994 involving whistles

shove ha'penny boards in Swaziland

small steps for a man ('One giant leap for mankind')

times the word 'girl' is in the King James Bible: 'And they have cast lots
    for my people; and have given a boy for an harlot, and sold a girl for
    wine, that they might drink.' (Joel 3:3)

under par for a birdie

US presidents born under the sign of Gemini (George Bush)

wheels on a unicycle

years' marriage for a cotton anniversary

The word 'one' has occurred in the titles of at least 500 films of which
the following are of particular note:

One A.M. (1914): a drunken Charlie Chaplin spends twenty minutes
    trying to climb the stairs to bed

Johnny One-Eye (1950): Pat O'Brien in a Damon Runyon story

Number One (1969): Charlton Heston as an aging football player

One Day in the Life of Ivan Denisovich (1971): Tom Courtenay in the
    title role of this Solzhenitsyn adaptation

One is a Lonely Number (1972): drama based on a story *The Good Humor
    Man* by Rebecca Morris

The Magnificent One (1974): Jean-Paul Belmondo in a James Bond spoof

1 = 2? (1975): French comedy

One Flew Over the Cuckoo's Nest (1975): Jack Nicholson in the multiple
    Oscar-winning film of Ken Kesey's book

Capricorn One (1978): O. J. Simpson turns up in this tale of NASA
    faking a Mars landing

One Trick Pony (1980): written and scored by Paul Simon

Duet for One (1986): Julie Andrews and Max von Sydow in a drama
    about a violinist

And before they go astray, we must mention four more:

One of Our Aircraft is Missing (1941)

One of Our Spies is Missing (1966)

One of Our Dinosaurs is Missing (1975)

One of My Wives is Missing (1976)

The number one also occurs in a wide range of idiomatic expressions
including: one-armed bandit, one foot in the grave, one-horse town, one-

night stand, one-track mind, one-way street, one-way ticket, one-man-band and one fell swoop.

■ 2

'There are two sides to every question.'
Protagoras, Greek philosopher and sophist of the fifth century BC, believed to have been the first person to study and write on grammar.

While the Greeks objected with intensity to thinking of one as a number, they were difficult about two as well. It was a perfectly good number in many respects, and useful for counting and multiplying in a way that one was not, but they still had reservations. Two could be said to have a beginning and end, but no middle. The geometers in particular felt that two did not fulfil the required standards: you can have a perfectly good three-sided figure, but a two-sided one falls flat.

Two, in religious mysticism, is the number of disunity and the number of creation – because two represents the splitting apart of divine unity. It is, perhaps, no coincidence that both the Old Testament and the Koran begin, in their original languages, with the second letter of the alphabet: *b'reshit* (In the beginning) and *bismillah* (In the name of God).

Linguistically, two is associated with the prefixes bi- (Latin) and di- (Greek), though sloppiness creeps in with words such as bicycle (Latin two, Greek wheels) and bigamy (Latin two, Greek marriages) which ought to be dicycle and digamy. A more hidden two is found in the word 'diploma', which is a certificate folded in two. Also several words beginning tw- reflect the number two: a twig is where a branch splits into two; twine is a rope formed by plaiting two threads together. One word that has no etymological connection with two-ness is 'bikini', named after the Pacific atoll where nuclear tests were held. The suitability of the apparent bi- prefix, however, led to the later words 'monokini' and 'trikini' for one- and three-piece swimsuits.

Two is also the number of:
bottles in a magnum
Gentlemen of Verona
kilograms minimum weight for a man's discus
nickels in a dime
pipes in a tun
places on earth named 'Hell', one in Norway, the other in the Cayman
  Islands

recorded accidents in the home in the UK in 1994 involving kitchen
    scales
shots under par for an eagle at golf
teaspoons in a dessertspoon, and dessertspoons in a tablespoon though
    British spoons and American spoons appear to differ in size: in North
    America a teaspoon is officially 4.833 millilitres and equals one third
    of a tablespoon; in Britain a teaspoon is 3.625 millilitres and is a
    quarter of a tablespoon
times Princess Diana uttered the name 'Charles' during her hour-long
    Panorama interview on television in 1995
times the word 'cheese' is in the King James Bible
turtle doves my true love gave to me

wrongs that don't make a right
years' marriage for a paper anniversary

The word 'two' has turned up in the titles of some 300 films including
the following:
The Man with Two Faces (1934): Edward G. Robinson in a crime
    mystery
Breakfast for Two (1937): Barbara Stanwyck comedy romance
Two Sisters from Boston (1946): musical with Jimmy Durante
The Two Mrs Carrolls (1947): Humphrey Bogart and Barbara Stanwyck
    in a tale of a serial wife-killing artist
Eagle With Two Heads (1948): Jean Cocteau romance
A Kid for Two Farthings (1955): David Kossoff stars in an adaptation of
    Wolf Mankowicz's novel
Only Two Can Play (1962): loose adaptation of Kingsley Amis's *That
    Uncertain Feeling*, with Peter Sellers
Two for the Seesaw (1962): Shirley MacLaine and Robert Mitchum in a
    comedy romance

Flat Two (1962): Edgar Wallace mystery

Two for the Road (1967): Albert Finney and Audrey Hepburn in a story by Frederick Raphael

The Magnificent Two (1967): Morecambe and Wise comedy

Two Mules for Sister Sara (1970): Clint Eastwood and Shirley MacLaine in nineteenth-century Mexico

The Incredible Two-Headed Transplant (1971): low-budget horror

Two English Girls (1972): François Truffaut adaptation of a novel by Henri-Pierre Roche

Two Against the Law (1973): Alain Delon and Jean Gabin

Number Two (1975): experimental film about a constipated wife and impotent husband

2 Catch 2 (1979): drama about a gambler's high-risk attempt to recoup his losses

Chapter Two (1979): James Caan and Marsha Mason in adaptation of Neil Simon's stage hit

The Man With Two Brains (1983): Steve Martin and Sissy Spacek in sci-fi spoof

Two Men and a Wardrobe (1985): Roman Polanski slapstick

A Zed and Two Noughts (1985): decaying matter beautifully filmed by Peter Greenaway

■ 3

'What I tell you three times is true.'
Lewis Carroll, *The Hunting of the Snark*, 1876

Good things come in threes: animal, vegetable and mineral; solid, liquid and gas; gold, silver and bronze medals; ego, id and superego; reading, writing and arithmetic; God the Father, Son and Holy Ghost. Three is the first number that all Greeks were able to agree was worthy of the term 'number'. As Aristotle pointed out, it is the lowest number to which the term 'all' can properly be applied. And three repairs the damage that two did, in splitting things apart.

Numerically, three is the second triangular number: $3 = 1+2$; the next triangular number is 6 which is $1+2+3$, then 10 $(1+2+3+4)$ and so on. Imagine a single point with two points below it, three below them, four below them and so on, forming an ever-growing triangle and you will see where the name comes from. Anyway, in 1796, Gauss, at the age of nineteen, proved that every number is the sum of at most three triangular numbers.

Linguistic triples begin with tri- in both Greek and Latin derivations. Three of the less obvious are 'trivial' – meaning three roads, indicative of the sort of talk you get at crossroads; 'tripos' – which refers not to three parts of an examination but to the three legs of the stool on which the examiner sat; and 'trilogy' – which ought really to mean three words, not three books.

Three is also the number of:
baths taken by Louis XIV in his entire lifetime
blind mice
days Jonah spent in the belly of the whale
dimensions of the physical world
Fates: Lachesis (who determined the fate), Clotho (spinner of thread of life), Atropos (who cut the thread)
feet in a yard
French hens my true love gave to me
Furies: Alecto (the unresting), Megaera (the jealous), Tisiphone (the avenger)
garden hoes in the traditional dowry for a wife in Rwanda
Graces (Aglaia, Thalia, Euphrosyne – the daughters of Zeus and Eurynome)
highest number in the language of the Yancos tribe of the Amazon: their word for three is 'Poettarrarorincoaroac'
highest number of overcoats found in the stomach of a single shark
illegitimate children of Friedrich August I of Saxony (King Augustus II of Poland) who became field marshals
injuries recorded in Britain in 1993 caused by accidents involving tea cosies
little maids from school in Gilbert and Sullivan's *Mikado*: (Yum-Yum, Peep-Bo, Pitti-Sing)
little pigs (and one big bad wolf)
Musketeers (Athos, Porthos, Aramis)
oranges in *The Love for Three Oranges* (opera by Prokofiev)
ounces of protein eaten per head daily in UK
people per square kilometre in Canada
primary colours: red, yellow and blue
recorded accidents in the home in the UK in 1994 involving weights for kitchen scales
sheets in the wind
Stooges (Larry, Moe and Curly)
Strikes and You're Out
teeth of his own that Stalin had left at his death
theological virtues: Faith, Hope and Charity
times Philip IV of Spain is said to have smiled in his life
under par for an albatross at golf

wheels on a tricycle

Wise Men (Gaspar, Melchior, Balthasar)

Wise Monkeys (Apes of Nikko: Mizaru, Mikazaru, Mazaru – see, hear and speak no evil)

witches in *Macbeth*

words in English still taking the old -en in the plural: oxen, brethren, children

years' marriage for a leather anniversary

Among the many films featuring the number three are the following:

The Three Musketeers (1916): Walt Whitman in a silent film adaptation of the classic

The Three Ages (1923): Buster Keaton silent comedy

These Three (1936): Merle Oberon in an adaptation of a play by Lillian Hellman

Three Faces West (1940): John Wayne beats the bad guys again

The Three Caballeros (1945): Donald Duck teams up with a parrot and a rooster

Three Strangers (1946): Sidney Greenstreet and Peter Lorre in a tale of gambling and violence

The Three Godfathers (1948): Peter Kyne's *Three Godfathers* was filmed five times, with John Wayne, in this version, the only one of the fifteen Godfathers to survive

A Letter to Three Wives (1949): Kirk Douglas in a tale of suspected infidelity

A Letter to Three Husbands (1950): Emlyn Williams in a tale of suspected infidelity

Soldiers Three (1951): Stewart Granger, Robert Newton and David Niven in a tale of the British army in India, loosely based on Kipling

Three Coins in the Fountain (1954): double Oscar-winning musical

The Three Faces of Eve (1957): psychodrama that won an Oscar for Joanne Woodward

Three Men in a Boat (1958): Jimmy Edwards, Lawrence Harvey and David Tomlinson in the film of Jerome K. Jerome's book

Three Moves to Freedom (1960): Claire Bloom and Curt Jurgens in an adaptation of Stefan Zweig's *The Royal Game*

The 3 Worlds of Gulliver (1960): adaptation of Jonathan Swift

The House of the Three Girls (1961): Austrian tale of unrequited love based on the life of Schubert

Threepenny Opera (1962): Sammy Davis Sr, Gert Frobe and Curt Jurgens in the opera by Berthold Brecht and Kurt Weill

The Three Lives of Thomasina (1963): adaptation of a Paul Gallico novel

The Three Sisters (1965): Geraldine Page and Shelley Winters in the film of Chekhov's play

Three Faces of a Woman (1965): Michelangelo Antonioni directs Richard Harris

Three (1969): Charlotte Rampling in a love triangle

Three Into Two Won't Go (1969): Rod Steiger falls for Judy Geeson

The Three Sisters (1974): with Laurence Olivier, Joan Plowright, Derek Jacobi and Alan Bates

Three Days of the Condor (1975): Max von Sydow and Faye Dunaway in an adaptation of James Grady's book, *Six Days of the Condor*

Three Women (1977): Robert Altman directs Shelley Duvall and Sissy Spacek in psychodrama

Agatha Christie's *Murder in Three Acts* (1986): Peter Ustinov finds the murderer at Tony Curtis's parties

Three Men and a Baby (1987): Ted Danson, Steve Guttenberg and Tom Selleck babysit

Three Men and a Cradle (1985): the French original of the above

Three Men and a Little Lady (1990): the Baby grows up

The Three Musketeers (1993): Tim Curry is Richelieu in the latest adaptation

■ 4

'Four legs good, two legs bad.'
George Orwell, *Animal Farm,* 1945)

Four is the only number equal to the number of letters in its English word. The same applies in German, as *vier* has four letters, but there is no number-word in French that equals its number of letters, though Spanish and Russian have *cinco* (five) and *tri* (three) respectively. The Greeks, of course, did not know this, but they did associate the number four with earthly balance. Earth, air, fire and water were supposedly the elements out of which everything was composed; there were four humours which combined to produce a person's temperament; and north, south, east and west were the four points of the compass from which the Four Winds could blow you to any of the four corners of the earth.

In other cultures, the number four may have less positive overtones. In 1995 Taipei allowed residents to delete '4' from street numbers because it sounds like 'death' in Chinese. For the same reason the previous year they issued car number plates excluding the number 4. Many hospitals in China do not have a fourth floor.

Mathematically, there are a number of important theorems associated with the number four, none more intriguing that the Four-Colour Problem. The question, first posed in the middle of the nineteenth century, concerned how many colours you need to colour a map with the sole criterion being that no two areas (countries or counties, for example) sharing a common stretch of border may be the same colour. Many trials failed to produce any map, however complicated, that required more than four colours, yet for more than a century nobody could prove that four was always sufficient. The problem was finally solved in 1976 when the general theorem was proved except for a large number of possibly anomalous cases, and a computer was set to work for several weeks eliminating all the possible exceptions.

Linguistically, four is the number where the sequence once, twice, thrice comes to a stop. Foursomes may be indicated by the prefixes quadr- (Latin) or tetra- (Greek). Purists, therefore, were not surprised that when record companies in the 1960s launched 'quadraphonic' recordings the new technology met with an unreceptive market. It should, of course, have been called 'quadrasonic' or 'tetraphonic'.

Rude words traditionally have four letters and, according to the evidence of *Chambers Dictionary*, this reputation is well justified. Of the words listed in the dictionary as 'vulg' there are 22 with four letters compared with five of three letters (or six if you include an Americanism), ten of five letters, two of six and only one each of 7, 8, 9, 11 and 12 letters. The expression 'four-letter word', incidentally, dates back only to 1929. It must be mildly confusing for Francophones since the French for 'he let out a four-letter word' is, according to *Collins Dictionary*, 'il a sorti le mot de cinq lettres'.

Four is also the number of:
balls in croquet (blue, black, red, yellow)
bottles in a jeroboam
calling birds my true love gave me on the fourth day of Christmas
cups of tea drunk each day by the average Briton

THE CUP THAT CHEERS BUT NOT INEBRIATES.

dimensions of Einstein's space-time continuum

eggs eaten per week per capita in the UK

Evangelists – Matthew, Mark, Luke, John

fatal accidents in British homes caused by stationery/writing equipment
in 1992

fingers on each of Mickey Mouse's hands

freedoms mentioned by F. D. Roosevelt on 6 January 1941: speech and
expression; religion; from want; from fear

frogs eaten each year per capita in France

gates of Roman London, on the sites later known as Dourgate, Aldgate,
Aldersgate and Ludgate. In the seventeenth century, the walled city
could also be entered by Bishopsgate, Moorgate, Cripplegate and
Newgate. As well as these, there were the Postern Gate on Tower Hill
and Bridge Gate, but neither of those was an entry point through the
wall itself

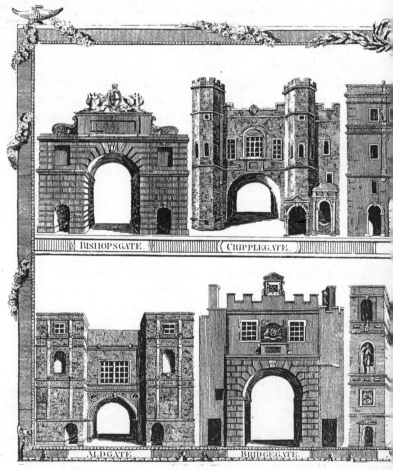

grams of salt in a litre of sweat
Honorary degrees held by Sammy Davis jnr
Horsemen of the Apocalypse: War, Famine, Pestilence, Death
humours: black bile, yellow bile, phlegm, blood
inches in a hand (when used as a measure of height for horses)
months an oyster can survive out of water
ounces of fat eaten per head daily
players in a game of whist or bridge – while whist takes its name, according to Cotton's *Complete Gamester* of 1680, from the 'silence that is to be observed in the play', the etymology of the name of the game of bridge (which dates back to around 1870) is unascertained, but it may be connected with a Slavonic word, *birritch*, meaning 'without trumps'
players on a polo team

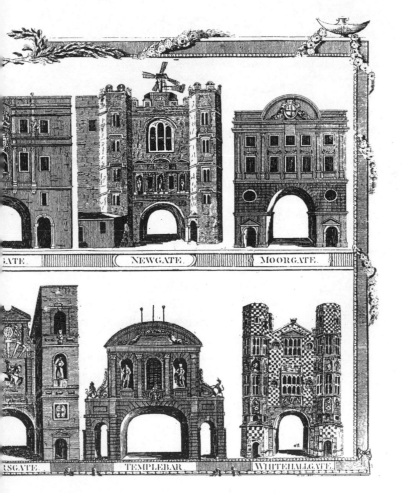

quarts in a gallon

recorded accidents in the home in the UK in 1994 involving thermostats

recorded accidents in the home in the UK in 1994 involving Christmas tree lights

riots at golf events in US 1960-72

roods in an acre

times Norway has scored 'nul points' in the Eurovision Song Contest

times the word 'Queen' occurs in the first verse of the National Anthem

toes on the front paw of the abominable snowman according to an alleged sighting in 1953

years' marriage for an iron (or some say fruit/flowers) anniversary

There are over a hundred films with the word or number four in the title, including the following:

The Four Horsemen of the Apocalypse (1921): with Rudolph Valentino doing the tango

Four Frightened People (1934): Claudette Colbert and Herbert Marshall in a Cecil B. de Mille drama

Four's a Crowd (1938): comedy with Errol Flynn and Olivia de Havilland

The Four Feathers (1939): love and cowardice in the desert with Sir Ralph Richardson, based on the book by A. E. W. Mason

The Four Just Men (1939): based on Edgar Wallace's book

Adam Had Four Sons (1941): Robert Shaw and Ingrid Bergman drama

4-D Man (1959): hokum in which scientist enters 4th dimension and goes mad

Four Days in November (1964): Kennedy assassination documentary

The Four Musketeers (1975): Michael York's d'Artagnan is upgraded for this sequel

The Four Seasons (1982): Alan Alda starred and directed

Mishima: A Life in Four Chapters (1985): biography of the writer Yukio Mishima who committed suicide after failing in a right-wing coup

Adventures of Sherlock Holmes – The Sign of Four (1985): Jeremy Brett as Holmes

Four Weddings and a Funeral (1994): very British romantic comedy

*'Five is the human soul. As man is a mixture of good and evil, so is
Five the first number made from both even and uneven.'*
Schiller: *Fünf ist des Menschen Seele. Wie der Mensch aus Gutem und
Bösem ist gemischt, so ist die Fünfe die ersten Zahl aus Grad' und
Ungerade* – from *Piccolomini*.

Five is an odd number, in both senses of the word. We have five fingers
on each hand, five toes on a foot and five senses; a starfish has five legs
and flowers frequently have five petals, yet true five-fold symmetry occurs
rarely in nature. The Pythagoreans, of course, had the answer: as the sum
of two (female) and three (male), five was the number of love and
marriage. Pythagoras's Theorem itself was sometimes known as the
'Theorem of the Bride', in recognition of the smallest right-angled
triangle with sides of integral length: three (male) and four (female)
containing the right-angle produced the offspring of a hypotenuse of
length five. Alternatively, you could add one (the number of divine
creation) to four (earthly balance) to get the answer five (the magic of
reproduction) – which may help to explain the supposed power of the
pentagram in magic. To complete the human connection, five is the
number of limbs, plus one for the body (or head).

Mathematically, five is the number of Platonic solids – the solid bodies
each of whose faces are congruent regular polygons: the tetrahedron
(whose four faces are all identical equilateral triangles); cube (six squares);
octahedron (eight triangles); dodecahedron (twelve pentagons); and
icosahedron (twenty equilateral triangles). Plato knew about all of them
and Euclid proved that there were no more than these five.

Since we are all told that our number system uses the base of ten
because we have ten fingers for counting on, it might seem legitimate to
wonder why we did not evolve a system of numbers to base five (perhaps
with the intention of leaving the other hand free for doing something
more useful than mere counting). In fact, the only language known to
have a counting system based on five rather than ten is Saraveca, one of
the Arawakan languages of South America.

Linguistically, sets of five are denoted by the prefix penta- (Greek) or
quin- (Latin). Quintets, quintuplets and pentathlons may be
quintessentially familiar, but most of us will have forgotten that
'quintessence' – the purest essential nature of something – is the fifth
essence, after earth, air, fire and water. The throat inflammation known
as quinsy, however, has nothing at all to do with the number five, but
comes from the Latin *quinancia*, which derives from the Greek *kynanche*
from *kyon*, dog + *anchein*, strangle, through whether it is supposed to

make you feel or sound like a dog being strangled is lost in etymological history.

Five is also the number of:
baseball gloves that can be made from one cow
Books of Moses comprising the Torah (or Pentateuch)
conductors needed for a performance of Henry Brant's *Antiphony 1*
fluid ounces in a gill
gold rings my true love gave me
Great Lakes of North America: Superior, Michigan, Huron, Erie and
    Ontario, of which Lake Michigan is the only one entirely in the
    United States
kilograms of sweets other than chocolate eaten per person per year in UK
magic beans in Jack and the Beanstalk
minutes it takes a good vet to castrate a cat
paintings by Picasso in the top ten most expensive sold at auction (the
    others comprise three by van Gogh and one each from Renoir and
    Jacopo da Carucci)
pints capacity of an average dog's stomach
recorded accidents in the home in the UK in 1994 involving strainers or
    sieves
recorded accidents in the home involving paperclips in 1994 in the UK
Rivers of Hades: Acheron (river of woe); Cocytus (lamentation); Lethe
    (oblivion); Phlegethon (fire); Styx (hate)
times the average British woman thinks about sex each day (according to
    a 1997 survey by *Cosmopolitan* magazine)
victories over enemy aircraft to quality to become an 'ace'
ways the letter 'f' may be pronounced in Icelandic
women named Mary in the New Testament
years it took Marva Drew of Waterloo, Iowa to type all numbers from 1
    to 1,000,000
years' marriage for a wood anniversary

Finally, we should mention a useful old saying: Spring has arrived when you can cover five daisies with your foot.

Over a hundred films have 'five' in the title including:
The $5 Counterfeiting Plot (1914): a six-minute silent film
Five Star Final (1931): Edward G. Robinson and Boris Karloff in a tale
    of journalistic immorality
Five Little Peppers and How they Grew (1939): children's story from the
    book by Margaret Sidney
The Beast with Five Fingers (1946): horror story from the book of the

same name by William Fryer Harvey

Five (1951): only five people survive a nuclear holocaust

The Sheep Has Five Legs (1954): classic French comedy with Fernandel in six roles

Five to One (1963): Dawn Adams and John Thaw in an Edgar Wallace crime story

Five-Card Stud (1968): Robert Mitchum and Dean Martin in a tale of poker and murder

Five Easy Pieces (1970): Jack Nicholson and Karen Black in a romantic drama

Slaughterhouse Five (1972): adaptation of Kurt Vonnegut's satirical novel

Five Fingers of Death (1973: martial arts epic which some say started the western Kung Fu craze

Five Miles to Midnight (1980): adventure with Joan Collins, Roger Moore and Tony Curtis

Dragon Lee vs the Five Brothers (1981): martial arts

Five Days One Summer (1982): romance and suspense with Sean Connery

Come Back to the Five and Dime, Jimmy Dean, Jimmy Dean (1982): Karen Black in a sex-change drama

■ 6

'Shakespeare never had six lines together without a fault. Perhaps you may find seven, but this does not refute my general assertion.'
Samuel Johnson

The number six has been imbued with great significance ever since God took that number of days to create the world. Mathematically, six is a perfect number (one that is equal to the sum of its proper divisors: 6 = 1+2+3), and St Augustine was among those who argued that God chose six days for the Creation precisely because six was perfect. Nature also finds the number six useful in its own creative processes, as may be seen in the hexagonal structure of the snowflake and the bees' honeycomb, and in the benzene ring, C_6H_6, the idea of which is said to have come to the German chemist Friedrich Kekulé von Stradonitz in a dream.

Mathematically, six is a triangular number (1+2+3) and a factorial (3×2×1) as well as being perfect. It is also the only number that is equal to the sum of exactly three of its own factors. Here's an old trick involving the number six: think of a non-zero number (9, for example), and multiply it by three (27). Count backwards two steps from the answer (27, 26, 25) and add all three numbers together

---

(27+26+25 = 78). Add together the digits of your answer (7+8 = 15) and do so again until you reach a single digit (1+5 = 6). The answer will always be six.

Linguistically, sixes are signified by hexa- (Greek) or sexa- (Latin). A semester was originally a term of six (Latin: *sex*) months (*menses*), and even the Spanish *siesta* began as a rest at the sixth hour of the day (around noon, if you get up early enough). A sextant is so called because its most basic design is to measure the arc that is a sixth part of a circle.

Six is also the number of:
bottles in a rehoboam
characters in search of an author in the Pirandello play
deaths caused by the Great Fire of London

feet in a fathom
geese-a-laying that my true love gave to me
ligulae (= 1/50 pint) in an acetabulum (= vinegar pot – now the socket of
    the hip joint) in Ancient Rome
men hanged for sodomy in England and Wales in 1806
men shaved in one minute by champion barber Robert Hardie in 1909
months in the life of the average American spent waiting for red lights to
    change
pints held by average ten-gallon hat
players on hockey team
radios in the average US household
ratio of the earth's gravity to the moon's
recorded accidents in the home in the UK in 1994 involving bidets

sides on a snowflake

toes Charles VIII of France had on one foot (having one more than the standard number of digits on hand or foot is known as hexadactylism). The West Indian cricketer Garry Sobers was born with a supernumerary finger on each hand, but this was corrected by an early operation

ways Shakespeare spelt 'Shakespeare'

wives of Henry VIII

years' marriage for a sugar anniversary

There are fewer than a hundred films with 'six' in the title. Here are some of them:

The Secret Six (1931): crime mystery with Clark Gable and Jean Harlow

Six Bridges To Cross (1955): crime drama with Tony Curtis and Sal Mineo – from a book by Joseph F. Dinneen called *They Stole $2,500,000 and Got Away With It*

Two and Two Make Six (1962): comedy drama

With Six You Get Egg Roll (1968): Doris Day comedy

6 Rms Riv Vu (1975): Alan Alda and Carol Burnett comedy

Six Weeks (1982): love story with Mary Tyler Moore and Dudley Moore

Six Degrees of Separation (1993): Sidney Poitier true-life drama

06 (1994): dirty Dutch film – 06 is the phone code for sex lines

And moving slightly ahead of six, we should mention that 'half-past six' is Singaporean English for not completely sane.

■ 7

'Wisdom hath builded her house, she hath hewn out her seven pillars.'
Proverbs 9:1

Adding the day of rest to the six days of creation, we arrive at the seven-day week and the most magically mystical number of all. In ancient Egypt there were seven paths to heaven. The ancient Babylonians had seven levels in their ziggurat, or step-pyramid, and their tree of life had seven branches, as also did the symbolic Jewish candlestick, the menorah. The ancient Chinese saw seven as the number governing female life: milk teeth arrive at seven months and fall out at seven years; puberty arrives at twice seven years and the menopause at seven times seven. The Old Testament is packed with sevens, from the seven times Cain's murder will be avenged to the seven days Noah's dove spent away from the ark, the seven steps leading to Solomon's temple (which took seven years to build), the seven locks of Samson, seven sneezes of a child raised from the dead by Elijah (2 Kings 4:35), and many others. The New Testament carries on the worship of heptads with the seven gifts of the holy spirit, seven last words of Christ on the cross and seven seals and seven trumpets in the Book of Revelation. By the time Shakespeare wrote of the seven ages of man the idea had already been firmly established for many centuries.

No wonder, then, that seven is associated with good luck, even in modern times. In Japan, for example, at seven minutes past seven, on the seventh day of the seventh month of the seventh year of the Japanese emperor's reign (1995), 17 runners ran 7,777 metres round the imperial palace, and all because the number seven is considered lucky. And that is also why we drink 7-Up and fly in Boeing aeroplanes known by a single digit sandwiched between two sevens.

Psychologically, seven is approximately the number of different things we can hold in our short-term memories at the same time. This idea was first expressed in 1956 in a paper by G. A. Miller entitled: 'The magical number seven plus or minus two: some limits on our capacity for processing information' (*Psychological Review*, vol 63, pp 81-97). Subsequent research has confirmed that our ability to remember strings of words, numbers or other items is generally limited to strings of between five and nine, depending on the complexity of each item, unless we have specially trained ourselves for a specific task such as remembering playing cards or series of digits.

Linguistically, sevens usually come in the two varieties of Greek, hepta- and Latin, septem-. Particular note should be taken of the word 'septemvious' meaning in seven different directions, of which the *Oxford English Dictionary* supplies only one usage, in 1861. Slightly more common, particularly in Oxford University, is the word 'hebdomadal' meaning once every seven days, hence once a week, which is how often the Hebdomadal Council meets.

Academically, a heptatechnist is a professor of the 'Seven Arts' (also known as the 'free' or 'Liberal' arts) a term first applied in the Middle Ages to a course of seven sciences, dating back to the sixth century, comprising grammar, logic and rhetoric (these three known as the *trivium*) as well as arithmetic, geometry, music, and astronomy (the *quadrivium*).

Seven is also the number of:
archangels in the earliest references
colours of the rainbow: red, orange, yellow, green, blue, indigo, violet
    (though there is good reason to believe that Isaac Newton added
      indigo to the list in 1704 only to make the number up to the magical
      seven)

deadly sins: lust, sloth, gluttony, envy, wrath, pride, avarice

Dwarfs encountered by Snow White: Sleepy, Happy, Dopey, Bashful, Grumpy, Sneezy, Doc

eclipses (lunar + solar) possible in a single year

grams a human eyeball weighs

Heavens in the Muslim religion: Silver, Gold, Pearl, White Gold, Silver & Fire, Ruby & Garnet, Divine Light Impossible for Mortal Man to Describe

Hills of Rome: Aventine, Caelian, Capitoline, Esquiline, Palatine, Quirinal, Viminal

length in feet of an average blue whale's penis

minutes length of a chukkah in polo

the pH value of pure water (less than seven = acidic, more than seven = alkaline)

the percentage of methane in a fart

Pillars of Wisdom of T. E. Lawrence

players on a netball team

recorded accidents in the home in the UK in 1994 involving a poker

recorded accidents in the home in the UK in 1994 involving tape measures

Seas: Antarctic, Arctic, N. Atlantic, S. Atlantic, Indian, N. Pacific, S. Pacific

Sisters (in North London)

Sisters (US Ivy League colleges)

Sisters (the Pleiades constellation of stars)

skeins in a hank

swans-a-swimming given by my true love

Virtues: Faith, Hope, Charity, Fortitude, Justice, Prudence, Temperance

voyages of Sinbad

Wonders of the Ancient World: Colossus of Rhodes, Pyramid of Cheops, Hanging Gardens of Babylon, Pharos Lighthouse of Alexandria, Mausoleum at Halicarnassus, Statue of Zeus at Olympia, Temple of Diana at Ephesus

years of age at which Chopin wrote his first polonaise

years' marriage for a wool anniversary

The magnificence of 'seven' has made it a popular number to appear on screen. Here are some of the titles:

Seven Chances (1925): Buster Keaton silent movie about a lawyer who will inherit $7m if he marries by 7pm

Bluebeard's Seven Wives (1926): silent film comedy

Snow White and the Seven Dwarfs (1937): Disney classic

The Door With Seven Locks (1940): Edgar Wallace horror story

The House of the Seven Gables (1940): Vincent Price and George Sanders in a faithful adaptation of Nathaniel Hawthorne's novel

Madonna of the Seven Moons (1945): based on a book of the same title by Margery Lawrence

Seven Keys to Baldpate (1947): Jason Robards in the film of the book by Earl Derr Biggers

The Seven Samurai (1954): Akira Kurosawa's classic tale starring Toshiro Mifune

Seven Brides for Seven Brothers (1954): Oscar-winning musical with Howard Keel

The Seven Year Itch (1955): Marilyn Monroe film from the play by George Axelrod

The 7th Voyage of Sinbad (1958): fantasy adventure

The Seven Hills of Rome (1958): musical with Mario Lanza

The House of the Seven Hawks (1959): Donald Wolfit and David Kossoff in a tale of Nazi treasure

The Magnificent Seven (1960): western remake of Kurosawa's *The Seven Samurai*

Robin and the Seven Hoods (1964): musical gangster comedy with Bing Crosby, Frank Sinatra and Dean Martin

Seven Days in May (1964): from the book of the same title by Fletcher Knebel and Charles W. Bailey

Return of the Magnificent Seven (1966): the first sequel, though only Yul Brynner returns

The Duck Rings at Half Past Seven (1969): German comedy

Guns of the Magnificent Seven (1969): sequel

The Magnificent Seven Deadly Sins (1971): Spike Milligan and Harry Secombe comedy

The Magnificent Seven Ride (1972): the final sequel

The Seven Brothers Meet Dracula (1974): martial arts vampire movie with Peter Cushing

The Seven Percent Solution (1976): Alan Arkin as Sigmund Freud, Nicol Williamson as Holmes and Sir Laurence Olivier as Moriarty in an adaptation of Nicholas Meyer's book

Dracula and the Seven Golden Vampires (1978): another martial arts vampire film with Peter Cushing

Seven (1979): gunslinger is paid $7m by the US government to deal with some gangsters

Seven Sixgunners (1987): western adapted from the book by Nelson Nye

Finally, let us not forget the name by which the secret ingredient of Coca-Cola is known: 7X

'And on the eighth day, the flesh of his foreskin shall be circumcised.'
Leviticus 12:3

Eight is an auspicious number through whichever religion you look at it. The Muslims believe in eight paradises (and seven hells): Christ, in his Sermon on the Mount, mentioned eight beatitudes; Buddhism teaches the noble eightfold path of enlightenment (right understanding, right aspiration, right speech, right conduct, right means of livelihood, right endeavour, right mindfulness and right contemplation); and Norse mythology gave Odin an eight-legged horse called Sleipnir and a ring, Draupnir, from which eight rings of equal value dropped off every nine days.

Mathematically, 8 is the cube of 2. It is also one less than 9, making it the only cube that is one less than a square.

Linguistically, we have the curious phrase 'one over the eight', meaning drunk, with its implication that any reasonable person can down eight pints of beer without ill effects, but no more. Whether from Greek or Latin, eightsomes are indicated by the prefix oct- (as in 'octopus', of which the plural is 'octopuses' or 'octopodes', but definitely not 'octopi'). Strictly, words derived from the Greek ought to begin octa- with Latin ones starting octo-, but evidence of this has almost totally vanished. Here is an octad of more unusual oct- words listed in the *Oxford English Dictionary*: octaeterid (an eight-year period in the ancient Greek calendar), octarchy (government by eight rulers), octodactyl (eight-fingered), octoceratous (eight-horned), octodentate (eight-toothed), octogamy (marrying eight wives), octoglot (written in eight languages), octophthalmous (eight-eyed). The 'high octane' petrol you buy also refers to the eight carbon atoms in paraffin of the octacarbon series C_8H_{18}.

Eight is also the number of:
bits in a byte in computer-speak
bottles in a methuselah
days in an ancient Roman week – seven working, one market
English kings named Henry
feet in length of the largest normal koala's appendix
furlongs in a mile
kilograms of chocolate eaten per person per year in UK
legs on a spider
maids a-milking my true love gave to me
ounces weight of a professional boxing glove

the most mutton legs found in the stomach of one shark

pints in a gallon

qus (also spelt qs, ques or cues) in an old English penny – a vital piece of
information for no-holds-barred Scrabble players, although 'qu' and
'qs' are both excluded from the official Scrabble list of permitted two-
letter words

reals in a Spanish dollar or peso; the coin was marked with the figure '8',
hence the term 'pieces of eight'

reindeer of Santa Claus: Dasher, Dancer, Prancer, Vixen, Comet, Cupid,
Donner and Blitzen, first appearing in a poem 'A Visit from St
Nicholas' written by Clement Moore in 1822. The more famous
Rudolph was not created until 1939 in a story by Robert L. May

years' marriage for a bronze anniversary

Here are eight films with an eight in their titles:

Dinner at Eight (1933): John Barrymore, Lionel Barrymore and
Jean Harlow drama

Curtain at Eight (1934): murder in the theatre

Eight O'clock Walk (1954): Richard Attenborough as an English taxi
driver wrongly accused of murder

Eight Witnesses (1954): Dennis Price in a mystery where all the witnesses
to a murder are blind

Where Eight Bells Toll (1971): Jack Hawkins and Anthony Hopkins in an
Alistair MacLean thriller

Kung Fu of the Eight Drunkards (1980): martial arts

8 Men Out (1988): classic tale of baseball corruption

8 Seconds (1994): sports biopic

And let us not forget:

8½ (1963): Fellini's classic of love and art

'Nine worthies were they called, of different rites –
Three Jews, three pagans, and three Christian knights.'
Dryden, 'The Flower and the Leaf'

Dryden's Nine Worthies were Joshua, David and Judas Maccabeus:
Hector, Alexander and Julius Caesar; King Arthur, Charlemagne and
Godfrey of Bouillon. Nine is a popular number for such a list, for if good
things come in threes what can be better than three sets of three? We
meet another such nonad in Macaulay's 'Lays of Ancient Rome':

Lars Porsena of Clusium
By the nine gods he swore
That the great house of Tarquin
Should suffer wrong no more.

In this case, the reference was to the nine gods of the Etruscans: Juno,
Minerva and Tinia (the three main gods), together with Vulcan, Mars
and Saturn, Hercules, Summanus and Vedius. The nine lives of a cat,
nine tailors it takes to make a man, the stitch in time that saves nine and
the happiness of being on cloud nine are further examples of the
goodness of nineness. The number does, however, have a darker side,
with the ninth psalm foretelling the anti-Christ, and Christ himself dying
on the cross at the ninth house of the day (3 p.m. equals nine hours after
dawn). The word 'noon' originally meant this ninth hour, but was later
found to be more useful to designate the time we now know as midday.

Mathematically, a number is divisible by nine if and only if the sum of
its digits is divisible by nine. Nine is also three squared, and is the only
square that is the sum of two consecutive cubes: $9 = 3^2 = 1^3 + 2^3$.

Nine is also the number of:
babies born to nine-year-old mothers in England and Wales in 1980
circles of hell in the Divine Comedy
circumference in feet of the cheese made for Queen Victoria in 1841
     from a single milking of the 737 cows in Pennard, Glastonbury
gallons of saliva secreted daily by a horse
heads of the hydra, usually, though since Hercules found that two more
     grew for each one he cut off, the number was variable
hours it takes an army ant to walk a mile
ladies dancing that my true love gave to me
milligrams of rat droppings permitted in a kilo of wheat by the US Food
     and Drug Administration
Muses: Clio (history), Melpomene (tragedy), Thalia (comedy), Calliope
     (epic poetry), Urania (astronomy), Euterpe (lyric poetry), Terpsichore

(dance and choral song), Polyhymnia (song and oratory), Erato (love poetry)

planets in the solar system

points of the law, which according to Brewer comprise: a good deal of money; a good deal of patience; a good cause; a good lawyer; a good counsel; good witnesses; a good jury; a good judge; and good luck

recorded accidents in the home in the UK in 1994 involving sash cords

width in inches of a cricket wicket

words in the Solomon Islands for various stages of maturation of coconut

years' marriage for a copper anniversary

There are only about 30 films with 'nine' in their titles, including:

Nine Days a Queen (1934): Sybil Thorndike and Cedric Hardwicke in Story of Lady Jane Grey

The Man With Nine Lives (1940): Boris Karloff as a mad doctor

Nine Lives are Not Enough (1941): Ronald Reagan solves a murder

Nine Hours to Rama (1963): film of the book by Stanley Wolpert

Nine Days of One Year (1964): Russian drama about love, physics and radiation

9 to 5 (1980): Dolly Parton, Jane Fonda and Lily Tomlin plot revenge against male chauvinist boss

9½ Weeks (1986): Kim Basinger in a tale of erotic obsession

9½ Ninjas (1990): martial arts sex comedy

■ 10

'Could I come near your beauty with my nails,
I'd set my ten commandments in your face.'
William Shakespeare, *2 Henry VI*, 1592

The Pythagoreans had little doubt that ten was the most holy of all numbers. It was the sum of 1, 2, 3 and 4 and could thus be depicted as an equilateral triangle, known as the *tetraktys*, with one point at the apex, two arranged symmetrically below it, three below that and four along the base. With one representing existence, two creation, three life and four the elements from which everything is composed, ten just about summed up everything. All of which was, for the Pythagoreans, sufficient justification to explain the perfection of our having ten fingers and using that number as a base for our counting system ('Decadactylous', incidentally, is the word for 'having ten fingers'.) In recent times, the *tetraktys* has been more commonly associated with tenpin bowling.

Linguistically, any of the prefixes deca-, decem- (both Latin) or deka- (Greek) signify groups of ten. Most of those listed in the *Oxford English*

Dictionary relate to animals or plants, for example: decapterygious (ten-finned), decemcostate (ten-ribbed), decemdentate (ten teeth), decempedal (having ten feet, though once also used to mean ten feet long), decapetalous (ten petals) and decaspermal (producing ten seeds). For a fine example of the richness of the language, however, one could hardly do better than to have a choice between decaphyllous and decemfoliate, both of which mean having ten leaves. On a more human level, a ruling council of ten people is a decarchy.

Ten is also the number of:
acres in a square furlong
average duration in seconds of chimpanzees' intercourse
chromosomes of greenfly
Commandments
degrees Celsius of the average April temperature in London
enquiries about John Dillinger's penis received annually by the
    Smithsonian Institution
events in a decathlon: 100m, 400m, 1500m, 110m hurdles, long jump,
    high jump, pole vault, shot-put, discus, javelin
fathoms in a chain
grams in our average daily salt intake
heliports in the UK
feet high a basketball ring should be
lords a-leaping my true love gave to me
passengers on Boeing's first commercial passenger plane, the 247
Plagues of Egypt (Exodus 7-12): water becomes blood, frogs, lice, flies,
    cattle murrain, boils, hail and fire, locusts, darkness, slaying of first-
    born
platforms at Moorgate and Baker Street stations – the most on the
    London Underground
points on Mohs' scale of hardness: talc, gypsum, calcite, fluorite, apatite,
    felspar (or orthoclase), quartz, topaz, corundum, diamond
vowels in the Korean alphabet
years' marriage for a tin anniversary
years of age for the age of consent in England in 1576

Among the films that include 'ten' in their titles are:
The Ten Commandments (1923): Cecil B. de Mille directs a cast of
    thousands in this silent epic
Ten Days That Shook the World (1927): Eisenstein's epic silent film of the
    Russian Revolution
Ten Nights in a Bar-Room (1931): the perils of alcohol
Kate Plus Ten (1938): crime story from the book by Edgar Wallace

27 amendments to the US constitution

The Ten Commandments (1956): Charlton Heston as Moses
Ten North Frederick (1958): based on the novel by John O'Hara
Garlic is as Good as Ten Mothers (1960): educational video
Under Ten Flags (1960): Van Heflin and Charles Laughton wartime drama
10th Victim (1965): cult-sci-fi classic with Ursula Andress and Marcello Mastroianni
A Boy Ten Feet Tall (1965): children's movie with Harry H. Corbett and Edward G. Robinson
Ten Little Indians (1965): based on Agatha Christie's play *Ten Little Niggers*
10 Rillington Place (1971): life of the murderer John Christie
Ten Days Wonder (1972): Orson Welles in an Ellery Queen mystery
Hitler: The Last Ten Days (1973): with Alec Guinness as Hitler
Ten Little Indians (1975): the remake with Herbert Lom, Richard Attenborough and Charles Aznavour
10 (1979): starring Dudley Moore, Bo Derek and Ravel's Bolero

■ **11**

'At eleven o'clock he has his "elevenses", consisting of coffee, cream, more bread and more butter.'
P. G. Wodehouse, *Meet Mr Mulliner*

The derivation of the word 'eleven' is unknown, though some suggest it may come from the Aryan root *leiq* or *leip* meaning 'leave', on the tenuous grounds that eleven leaves you with one over, once you have counted up to ten. Another fact that has never been properly explained about eleven is why it is the number of players in a team for both Britain's major sports, cricket and soccer. One highly dubious explanation is that eleven, being one more than the holy number ten, is a reminder of the imperfection of mankind, especially when playing games. 'Eleven is sin; eleven transgresses the Ten Commandments,' wrote Schiller.

A more righteous side of eleven is reflected in the Dionysiads, a group of eleven women in Ancient Sparta formed to battle against the excesses of the Dionysian cult, and in the undecimvir, a panel of eleven Magistrates that sat in Ancient Athens. Undecim- is the prefix for anything to do with eleven, as in the words undeciman (or undecimarian) referring to church services that began at eleven o'clock, and undecimarticulate, having eleven sections or segments.

A modern though little realised example of undecimal counting is seen in the ISBN of published books. (It is, of course, a solecism to say 'ISBN number', since the N stands for 'Number' itself. The other letters are International Standard Book.) Any ISBN comprises ten digits. If you multiply the first by ten, the second by nine, the third by eight, and so on, summing the results as you go along, the result will always be divisible by eleven. This is a neat trick to guard against entering the wrong numbers on a computer. Any computer programmed to deal with ISBNs will perform the check automatically and stand a good chance of detecting any mistake. If you want to try this out on some of your own books, it may save time to remember the little test for divisibility by eleven: add the first, third, fifth and other odd digits of the number being tested and subtract the sum of the digits in the even places. If the result is divisible by eleven, then so is the number you started with.

Eleven is also the number of:
airports in Albania, of which only five have paved runways
the Apollo 11 spacecraft from which Neil Armstrong walked on to the
    moon
cups of coffee drunk daily per capita in Sweden – the world's most
    prolific coffee-drinkers
days lost in 1752 (3-13 September) on changing from the Julian to the
    Gregorian calendar (→365)
golden hamster babies in an average litter
hurricanes in the world in 1995 – highest since records began
Oscars won by *Ben Hur* – the most for any film
ounces in weight the average person loses overnight
pipers piping my true love gave to me
players in a soccer, netball, hockey or cricket team
recorded accidents in the home in the UK in 1994 involving drinking
    straws
riots at horse races in US between 1960 and 1972
states in the Confederacy

years' marriage for a steel anniversary

The films with 'eleven' in their titles include:
Eleven Men and a Girl (1930): US football romance
Ocean's Eleven (1960): Shirley MacLaine, Frank Sinatra and Dean
    Martin comedy caper
11 Harrowhouse (1974): comedy-crime caper with Trevor Howard,
    James Mason, Sir John Gielgud and Candice Bergen

'At twelve noon, the natives swoon, and no further work is done.'
Noel Coward, *Mad Dogs and Englishmen*

From the twelve months of the year to the twelve signs of the zodiac; from the twelve tribes of Israel to the twelve apostles of Christ, the number twelve has a powerful influence in a wide range of myths and cultures. Divisible by two, three, four and six, twelve would surely form a better basis for a counting system, if we did not fall two fingers short. Yet the usefulness of twelve is clearly shown in the existence of the words 'dozen' and 'gross'.

The number twelve has a curious arithmetical property: the square of 12 is 144 which, oddly enough, is the reverse of the answer when you square the reverse of 12: 21 squared equals 441. The only other pair of numbers with a similar property are 13 and 31.

Linguistically, the prefix for a dozen of anything is dodeca- as in the twelve-faced dodecahedron and the twelve islands in the Dodecanese group in the Aegean. (Though the 'Twelve Apostles' island group in lake Superior comprises about twenty islands.)

The word 'twelve' is too old for anyone to know where it came from, but the initial tw- must have something to do with 'two'. Compared with 'eleven' the evidence is stronger that 'twelve' indicates 'two left' (when you have taken ten away). Brewer conjectures that at one time people had no need to count higher than twelve, so the numbers from one to twelve had distinctive names, with the -teen series introduced only when we had reached a 'more advanced state'.

Throughout the history of counting there have occasionally been suggestions that, in the spirit of easier divisibility, we ought to abandon the custom of counting to base ten and substitute numbers to base twelve. (So we would write twelve as 10, the number we now know as 24 would be 20 and the current 144 would be 100 in the new system.) In 1944, the Duodecimal Society of America was founded in order to campaign for such a change, and the Duodecimal Society of Great Britain followed in 1959. Both subsequently changed the 'Duodecimal' in their names to the simpler 'Dozenal'. Nevertheless, there were disputes about how to write the new numbers necessary to signify the old ten and eleven, and what to call them. The original proposal of the DSA was to have X for ten and E for eleven, but the British preferred to use 2 and 3 written upside down, which they borrowed from Sir Isaac Pitman's *Phonetic Journal.* Then the Americans changed to X and #. There have also been differences of opinion on the words to be used for the new numbers and whether the new '10' should be called 'ten' or 'one doz'.

Twelve is also the number of:

apostles, chosen by Jesus to spread his teachings after his death.
Originally they were: Andrew, Bartholomew (or Nathaniel), James
son of Alphaeus, James son of Zebedee, John, Jude (or Thaddeus),
Judas Iscariot, Matthew (or Levi), Philip, Simon Peter, Simon the
Zealot, and Thomas. After Judas's suicide, he was replaced by
Matthias. St Paul is also generally included, because of his claim to
have seen Jesus after the resurrection

Astrological Houses: Life, Fortune & Riches, Brethren, Parents &
Relatives, Children, Health, Marriage, Death, Religion, Dignities,
Friends & Benefactors, Enemies

bottles in a salmanazar

Days of Christmas

drummers drumming my true love gave to me

'filthy words' laid down by Federal Communications Commission in
1973: fuck, shit, piss, cunt, turd, twat, fart, ass, motherfucker,
cocksucker, tits, cock

gallons of saliva secreted daily by the average cow

grams of instant coffee consumed by the average Briton each week

hoops in croquet

inches in a foot

hours each month the average American spends in shopping malls

Labours of Hercules, performed to expiate his guilt after killing his wife
and children in a fit of madness. They were: killing the Nemean lion
and the Hydra of Lerna, capturing the Hind of Ceryneia and the Boar
of Erymanthus, cleaning the Augean stables, chasing away the
Stymphalian birds, capturing the Cretan bull and the horses of
Diomedes, stealing the girdle of Hippolyta capturing the oxen of
Geryon, stealing the apples of the Hesperides, and capturing and
binding Cerberus in Hades

letters in the Hawaiian alphabet
minutes a bedbug takes to feed
pairs of ribs of a human being
pence in an old shilling
people who have set foot on the moon
pints of blood in the average human body
points on the Mercalli Scale of Felt Intensity of earthquakes (from 1 –
    perceived only by sensitive instruments – to 12 – masses of rock
    displaced horizontally and vertically)
points on the original Beaufort scale
postal deliveries a day in London at the end of the nineteenth century
randomly tuned radios in John Cage's *Imaginary Landscape No. 4* (1953)
riots at motor sport events in US between 1960 and 1972
signs of the zodiac
square kilometres of Africa always covered in ice
tablets on which the 'Laws of the Twelve Tables' were inscribed. The
    first written laws of the Romans, they were fixed to the speaker's stand
    in the Forum
tons of jellybeans bought by the White House during Reagan Presidency
Tribes of Israel
tricks for a small slam in bridge
years' marriage for a silk (or fine linen) anniversary

Apart from *The Dirty Dozen* (1967), and *The Dirty Dozen: The Next
Mission* (1985), and *The Dirty Dozen: the Deadly Mission* (1987), and
The Dirty Dozen: The Fatal Mission (1988), the films that come in
twelves include:
Twelve Miles Out (1927): silent film of drama aboard a ship with Joan
    Crawford
Twelve O'clock High (1942): war film with Gregory Peck
Her Twelve Men (1954): based on a book *Miss Baker's Dozen* by Louise
    Baker about a teacher with thirteen mischievous boy pupils
Twelve Angry Men (1957): juryroom drama with Henry Fonda and Lee J.
    Cobb
The Twelve-Handed Men of Mars (1964): Italian sci-fi
The Twelve Chairs (1970): Mel Brooks's version of the Ilf and Petrov
    story

And look out for:
Play: *The Twelve-Pound Look* (1910) by J. M. Barrie
Book: *The Wind's Twelve Quarters* (1975) by Ursula Le Guin

'It was a bright cold day in April, and the clocks were striking thirteen.'
George Orwell, *1984*

Thirteen is widely considered to be an unlucky number, though the origins of that fear – correctly termed triskaidekaphobia – are unclear. In Christian tradition, fear of thirteen is usually linked to the number present at the Last Supper, though that superstition dates back only to the Middle Ages when thirteen-fear was already widely established in other cultures. The Babylonians were suspicious of thirteen, apparently through a feeling that the sun needed to be kept separate from the twelve zodiac signs. Old Norse mythology tells of a banquet in Valhalla at which Loki arrived as an uninvited guest, making the number up to thirteen, which resulted in the death of Baldur.

The 1894 edition of Brewer's *Phrase and Fable* tells us that 'the Turks so disliked the number that the word is almost expunged from their vocabulary' and 'the Italians never use it in making up their lotteries'. The wisdom of the Italians was confirmed more than a century later when, after the first year of the British National Lottery, the two numbers that had been least favoured by the draw turned out to be 13 and 39 (3×13) – though 26 (2×13) had done considerably better than average. Around the end of the nineteenth century, street numbers in Paris would always jump from 12 to 14, omitting the unlucky number, while blocks of flats in London tended to have the euphemistic 12A. Even as late as 1960 the newly-built Carlton Towers hotel in London's Knightsbridge considered it wise to jump directly from the 12th to the 14th floor.

Writing in the *Smithsonian Magazine* in 1987, Paul Hoffman estimated that fear of the number thirteen costs the United States 'a billion dollars a year in absenteeism, train and plane cancellations and reduced commerce on the thirteenth of the month'. In 1967, a group of thirteen Americans were reported to have launched a campaign to rid the country of triskaidekaphobia. Their first act was to rent a plot of land thirteen feet long for thirteen cents a month. One noted triskaidekaphobe was the composer Arnold Schoenberg (pioneer, incidentally, of twelve-tone music), who died, as he had predicted, at the age of 76 (7+6 = 13), supposedly on Friday the thirteenth (→688) at thirteen minutes to midnight.

French society used to support a group of noble gentlemen known as the *quatorziennes*, who made themselves available at short notice to attend any dinner party or other formal function at which exactly thirteen people had turned up. Others, however, have – for good reasons of their own – associated thirteen with good luck. King Louis XIII of France was so fond of the number that he married Anna of Austria when she was thirteen years old, while world chess champion Garry Kasparov was born on the thirteenth of the month, scored his first ever victory against his great rival Anatoly Karpov on the thirteenth of the month, and has scored particularly well in thirteenth games of world championship matches.

Thirteen is also the number of:
cards in a suit
Coca-Colas a day sold in first eight months of its existence at Jacob's pharmacy in Atlanta, Georgia
estimated percentage of Britons trying to slim
inches waist measurement decreed for ladies at court of Catherine de Medici
lines in a rondeau
original colonies of the US
pounds' weight loss of an average mother during childbirth
record number of Caesarian births by one woman
recorded accidents in the home in the UK in 1994 involving rubber bands or elastic
stripes on the American flag (one for each of the original colonies)
times the spoil from digging the Channel tunnel would fill Wembley stadium
tricks for a grand slam in bridge
years of age at which the average American develops a phobia
years' marriage for a lace anniversary

The ill-omened connotations of thirteen have made it a popular number in films, including the highly successful horror film, *Friday the Thirteenth* (1980) and its seven sequels. Other numbers include:

13 Washington Square (1928): silent crime/romance comedy

13 Rue Madeleine (1946): D-Day spy drama with James Cagney and E. G. Marshall

13 Lead Soldiers (1948): Bulldog Drummond story

The 13th Letter (1951): Michael Rennie is accused of having an affair with Charles Boyer's wife

13 West Street (1962): Alan Ladd and Rod Steiger in action drama based on book *The Tiger Among Us* by Leigh Brackett

The 13 Chairs (1970): Terry-Thomas and Orson Welles in Ilf and Petrov Russian folk tale (also filmed by Mel Brooks as *The Twelve Chairs*)

In a Year of Thirteen Moons (1980): sex-change drama by Rainer Werner Fassbinder

Thirteen at Dinner (1985): murder mystery with Faye Dunaway and Peter Ustinov

The Alamo: Thirteen Days to Glory (1987): Davy Crockett's last stand

The 13th Mission (1991) US soldiers fight their way out of an Asian jungle

■ 14

'I spent fourteen months at Magdalen College: they proved the fourteen months the most idle and unprofitable of my whole life.'
Edward Gibbon, *Memoirs of My Life*, 1796

Despite the decline and fall of Gibbon's time at Magdalen College, the number fourteen is generally considered propitious. The moon takes fourteen days to change from new to full, whence the significance of a fortnight. The words of a popular old German lullaby run: 'When at night I go to sleep, fourteen angels watch do keep,' which indicates the protective quality of fourteen. It was the ancient Egyptians, however, who seemed most interested in fourteen. The great god Osiris, judge of the dead and potentate of the kingdom of ghosts, was identified with the moon, so it should be no surprise to hear that he is represented by an eye at the top of fourteen steps. When he was killed by his brother, Set, Osiris was cut into fourteen pieces which were buried in different places, each bringing the blessing of fertility to a different region. The myth goes that Isis, who was both Osiris's sister and his wife, sought out the pieces in order to reunite them, and found all but one. The fourteenth piece, the mystical 'Talisman of Set', was Osiris's penis.

For the best mysticism involving the number fourteen, however, we must go the French kings. Louis XIV ascended the throne in 1643 (1+6+4+3 = 14), reigned for 77 years (7+7 = 14), died in 1715 (1+7+1+5 = 14) and, if we add his birth year (1638) to his death year, the answer is 3,353, again adding up to fourteen. Henri IV, on the other hand, was not an XIV himself, but he was the fourteenth king of France and his name, Henri de Bourbon, had fourteen letters. He was born on 14 December 1553 (1+5+5+3 = 14) and was assassinated on 14 May 1610 at the age of fifty-six, which is four times fourteen.

The correct term for a set of fourteen things is a tessaradecad, not to be confused with a tetradecapod, which is a creature with fourteen feet. A poem of fourteen lines we all know to be a sonnet, but only as long as it fulfils certain other strict conditions, such as one of a set of prescribed rhyming schemes and having ten syllables in every line. A fourteen-line poem that does not quite qualify as a true sonnet may be known as a decatessarad or a quatoirzain. A line containing fourteen syllables is known as a tessaradecasyllabon or, more simply, a fourteener.

There are fourteen pounds in a stone, which seems curious, since fourteen has neither the merit of being a round decimal number nor the convenience of allowing easy subdivision in a way that the twelve pence in a shilling or sixteen ounces in a pound would allow. The explanation lies in the ramshackle origins of English pre-metric weights and measures. A pound (derived from the ancient Roman *libra pondo*, pound in weight, from the first word of which the lb abbreviation originates) used to vary between twelve and twenty-seven ounces, depending on the commodity that was being weighed. The sixteen-ounce pound *aveir de peis* (of merchandise weight) was made standard for bulky commodities by Edward III. Since 1826 this has been the only legal pound. Meanwhile, however, a stone varied between eight and twenty-four pounds. The fourteen-pound stone was decreed as standard by a 1495 Act of Henry VII, but only when wool was being weighed. Even as late as 1835 an Act of William IV declared: 'By local Customs, the Denomination of the Stone Weight varies'. The whole system only finally attained some degree of order with the Weights and Measures Act of 1878.

Fourteen is also the number of:
countries bordering Russia
days an ant can survive underwater
days' incubation for measles
days' reign of Lady Jane Grey
impulse decisions made by average US supermarket shopper
inches in the length of an okapi's tongue

kisses in the novels of Jane Austen (four between females, four on the hand, two female to children, one given by a man to a lock of severed hair and three between man and woman)

maximum number of golf clubs permitted per player

mph speed limit for light locomotives under the Highways Act of 1896

news weeklies on sale in London in 1645

percentage of the world's sheep living in Australia

possible meanings of the expression 'make up', according to a 1933 book entitled *American Speech*

seconds it took Napoleon's surgeon, Baron Dominique Larrey, to amputate a leg

times Nuri as-Said served as prime minister of Iraq between 1930 and 1958

vernacular and independent tongues of Europe, according to a seventeenth century linguist named Howell

wattage of human brain in deep thought

weight of largest hen's egg in ounces

years' marriage for an ivory anniversary

years of age at which Rin-Tin-Tin died in 1932

Films and other works with fourteen in their titles include:

Fourteen Hours (1951): from a story by Joel Sayre called *The Man on the Ledge*. Grace Kelly made her screen debut in this film

The Fourteen (1973): youthful drama with Alun Armstrong

Flying Claw Fights Fourteen Dragons (1980): adventure

14 Going on 30 (1988): teenage romance comedy with Loretta Swit

Poetry: 'Fourteen Men' (1954) by Dame Mary Gilmore

37 plays by Shakespeare

'And fifteen arms went round her waist
(And then men ask "Are barmaids chaste?")
John Masefield, *The Everlasting Mercy*, 1911

The Germans used to have a measure called a 'Mandel', referring to a collection of fifteen small objects. The word means 'little moon' and refers to the fifteenth day in a lunar month when the moon reaches its full strength. In 1851 Sir Edward S. Creasy wrote 'The Fifteen Decisive Battles of the World' in which he listed the following as the most significant military battles in history:

1. The battle of Marathon (490 BC) when Miltiades, commanding 10,000 Greeks, defeated a Persian army of 100,000.
2. The battle of Syracuse (413 BC) when the Athenians were defeated with the loss of their entire fleet and 40,000 killed or wounded.
3. The battle of Arbela (331 BC) when Alexander the Great defeated Darius Codomanus.
4. The battle of Metaurus (207 BC) when Livius and Nero destroyed Hasdrubal's army, which had been sent to reinforce Hannibal.
5. The defeat of the Romans by Arminius and the Gauls in AD 9, thus establishing the independence of Gaul.
6. The battle of Chalons (AD 451), at which Attila was defeated.
7. The battle of Tours (AD 732), when the Saracens were defeated and Europe broke free of the Moslem influence.
8. The battle of Hastings (1066) when William the Conqueror defeated Harold II.
9. The battle of Orleans (1429) when Joan of Arc secured independence for France.
10. The defeat of the Spanish Armada in 1588.
11. The battle of Blenheim (1704), when Marlborough and Prince Eugene inflicted the first major defeat on the forces of Louis XIV.
12. The battle of Pultowa (1709) when Czar Peter routed the forces of Charles XII of Sweden, thus laying the basis for Russian power.
13. The battle of Saratoga (1777) in the American War of Independence, when a large British army under John Burgoyne was defeated by American troops under the command of Horatio Gates.
14. The battle of Valmy (1792) when Marshal Kellerman of France defeated the Duke of Brunswick.
15. The battle of Waterloo (1815) when Napoleon was defeated by Wellington.

Fifteen is also the number of:

babies in the biggest recorded litter by a ferret

blows by executioner to sever the head of Mary Queen of Scots

escalators at Baker Street tube – the most on any station of the London Underground

inches diameter of netball ring

inches height of pins in tenpin bowling

medals awarded to Audie Murphy, most decorated US soldier in World War II

men on a dead man's chest sung of in Robert Louis Stevenson's *Treasure Island*. He borrowed the 'Dead Man's Chest', incidentally, from Charles Kingsley, who used the phrase as the name of one of the Virgin Islands in his novel *At Last* which was published in 1871, ten years before *Treasure Island*

minimum number of checkouts in a hypermarket

minutes everyone will be famous, according to Andy Warhol

people per square kilometre in Finland

pieces on each side in backgammon

pounds of hydrogen in average human body

red balls in snooker

sets of beads (one large and eleven small in each set) on a rosary, traditionally connected with fifteen mysteries of the life of Mary

years of age of Sheridan's bashful maiden: 'Here's to the maiden of bashful fifteen' (*The Rivals*)

years of the Fifteen Years' War between Austria and the Ottoman Turks from 1591 to 1606

years' marriage for a crystal anniversary

The films and other works with 'fifteen' in their titles include:

15 Maiden Lane (1936): crime feature with Cesar Romero

Angels One Five (1954): war drama

Poetry: 'Fifteen Dead' (1979), by Thomas Kinsella

And let us not forget that every 15 seconds, someone somewhere in Britain starts to dig a hole in the road

16

'Anni? Sedecim. Flos ipsus.'
Terence (Publius Terentius Afer) *c.*160 BC
(*Age? Sixteen. The very flower of youth.*)

Sixteen is the fourth power of two, which is why computers find it so useful as a base for counting. Indeed, much computer code is written in hexadecimal notation, with the digits from zero to nine augmented by the letters A to F. In the nineteenth century, J. W. Mystrom suggested that life would be easier if we all counted using base sixteen. Instead of one, two, three and so on, he proposed renaming the numbers an, de, ti, go, su, by, ra, me, ni, hu, vy, la, po, fi, ton. The idea, however, never caught on.

The delights of sixteen were appreciated by the ancient Romans, whose measuring system had four fingers to a hand and four hands to a foot. Thus there were sixteen fingers to the foot. The ancient Indians also thought well of the number, listing sixteen parts of a complete human, sixteen signs of beauty and sixteen pieces of jewellery adorning a perfectly bejewelled lady.

The Pythagoreans were fond of sixteen, as it is the only number that measures the perimeter and area of the same square.

The number also has a role to play in some European languages. Just as the counting systems in English (and German) change gear after twelve and start systematically adding -teen or -zehn to create higher numbers, the French and Italians persist with original number names until 16 (*seize, sedici*), before adopting the more consistently formulaic (*dix-sept, diciasette*) style for the remaining teens.

Sixteen is also the number of:
the amendment to the US constitution that introduced Federal Income
    Tax in 1913
annas in a rupee in India until recently
arms of the goddess Pussa
bottles in a balthazar
centimetres length of the average erect penis
chromosomes of the honey bee

countries bordering China
days in the gestation period of a golden hamster
drams in an ounce, ounces in a pound
eggs in the egg-purse of a cockroach
feathers in the tail of a red or spotted grouse
language groups of the 133 Italian tribes recognised in Mexico in 1914
mingles in a stekamen (Dutch liquid measure of the eighteenth century)
murders in Atlanta during Olympic Games in 1996
orders of mammals
pages the Pentagon's Dept of Food Procurement takes to define plastic
    whistles
parts of a complete human according to the Chandgya Upanishad
percentage of world's silver from Mexico
pounds weight minimum for a shot used in shotputting
rules in Esperanto
signs of beauty in classical Indian aesthetics
stitches in an embroiderer's eye stitch – all entering a single hole, but
    spread into a square on the outside edge
syllables in each line of a sloka – a couplet of Sanskrit verse
violin concertos by Vivaldi that Bach arranged for harpsichord
years you have to be married for there to be no metal or other substance
    conventionally associated with the anniversary – you must now wait
    four more years (→20) for a piece of china

Films and other works that celebrate the number sixteen include:
Sixteen Fathoms Deep (1948): from a story by Eustace Adams called
    Sixteen Fathoms Under
Sixteen (1972): coming-of-age story of girl from the deep south
Sweet Sixteen (1983): psychic horror with Bob Hoskins and Susan
    Strasberg
Song: 'Sweet Little Sixteen' (1958) by Chuck Berry

And let us not forget Sixteen-string Jack, alias John Rann, an eighteenth-century highwayman. He wore sixteen tags, eight at each knee and his stylish, if foppish manner even aroused the admiration of Samuel Johnson: 'Dr Johnson said that Gray's poetry towered above the ordinary run of verse as Sixteen-string Jack above the ordinary foot-pad.' (Boswell, *Life of Johnson.*) His career came to a sad end when he was hanged in 1774.

'I kiss'd her slender hand,
She took the kiss sedately;
Maud is not seventeen
But she is tall and stately.'
Tennyson, *Maud,* 1855

If you are searching for a mystical significance of the number seventeen, you need look no further than the Great Flood in the Book of Genesis, which began on the seventeenth day of the second month and ended on the seventeenth day of the seventh month. The watery nature of seventeen is also reflected in Greek legend, for that is the number of days Odysseus floated on a raft after leaving Calypso. Perhaps because of this the Greeks considered seventeen to be an unlucky number. (See 153 for further symbolism connected with the number seventeen.)

If you cube the number 17 you get 4,913, which, if you add its digits together, gets you back to 17. The only other numbers that are equal to the sum of the digits of their cubes are 1, 8, 18, 26 and 27.

Seventeen is also the number of:
bottle banks in UK in 1977 (the number had risen to over 13,000 by 1994)
children produced by Queen Anne
consecutive draws played by Anatoly Karpov and Garry Kasparov in their world chess championship match in 1984
feet width of a badminton singles court
goldfish bowls left on public transport in Tokyo in 1979
inches of human bottom allowed in the specification for seat width for British Rail
Italians expelled from Great Britain 1907-14 for prostitution and procuring
laughs a person has each day on average
the line of latitude dividing N. and S. Vietnam
most bananas eaten in two minutes
muscles controlling a dog's ear
pages the Pentagon's Dept of Food Procurement takes to describe olives
points on the Beaufort Scale of wind strength since 1955
the Seventeen Article Constitution, Japan's first known written law, introduced by Prince Shotoku in 604
syllables in a haiku – which probably stems from an ancient Japanese belief that seventeen is the optimum number of syllables spoken in a single breath

times James Boswell suffered from gonorrhoea
tons of gold made into wedding rings each year in US
tributaries of the River Severn

Seventeen is a rare visitor to film titles, with these two among the
exceptions:
Number Seventeen (1932): early Hitchcock jewel-robbery drama
Seventeen (1940): comedy based on the book *Seventeen* (1916) by Booth
   Tarkington

■ 18

'I've had eighteen straight whiskies – I think that's the record.'
Allegedly the last words of Dylan Thomas, 1953

Eighteen was a mystic number for the Mevlevi – the Sufi order of
whirling dervishes – whose apprenticeship included learning the eighteen
different kinds of service in the kitchen. It is also the age at which
adulthood traditionally begins and is thus when, in England and Wales
at any rate, you can sign a cheque, buy a house, buy and drink alcohol,
serve on a jury, have a credit card, get married without parental consent,
make a will and be hanged.
   We have already mentioned that eighteen is equal to the sum of the
digits in its cube (5,832), but the number exhibits a unique property if
we move on to its fourth power (104,976). For 18^3 and 18^4 together
utilise each of the digits from 0 to 9 once each.
   Linguistically, 'eighteen-wheeler' is CB-radio speak for a juggernaut.

Eighteen is also the number of:
the Amendment to US constitution introducing Prohibition
feet in the diameter of the pitchers' circle in baseball
French kings called Louis
haircuts performed in sixty minutes by Southampton hairdresser Trevor
   Mitchell to set a new record on 28 October 1996
holes on a golf course
inches in a cubit, approximately, though the length varied as it was
   defined as the distance from an individual's elbow to the tip of his
   middle finger
inches in one mkono (E. African unit of length)
inches in the diameter of a basketball ring
islands in the Faeroes
known satellites of Saturn
letters in the words 'conversationalists' and 'conservationalists', the
   longest pair of anagrams (excluding scientific terms) in English

43 years record of the Empire State Building

pairs of ribs of a horse
people in UK per personal computer bought in 1994
players in an Australian Rules football side
pounds in the record weight of a brussels sprout
Russians and Poles expelled from Great Britain 1907-14 for prostitution
    and procuring
Things known by Odin

times 'dog' appears in the Bible
tons of smoked salmon eaten at Wimbledon 1990
weeks at number one for Frankie Laine's 'I Believe'

Eighteen is also the age at which one can go to see any film in the
cinema, which may account for its popularity in film titles including:
Under Eighteen: (1932): teenage romance with Regis Toomey
Nearly Eighteen (1943): comedy
Eighteen and Anxious (1957): love and disappointment in Las Vegas
18 in the Sun (1964): teenage romance
18 Again! (1988): George Burns as an 81-year-old who exchanges souls
    with his 18-year-old grandson

And look out for:
Eighteen Poems (1934), the first published book by Dylan Thomas –
    which sums up his career rather neatly: from eighteen poems to
    eighteen whiskies.

'At nineteen, you know, one does not think very seriously.'
Jane Austen, *Emma*, 1815

Nineteen years is the period of the Metonic cycle, named after the Greek astronomer Meton, who discovered it in 433 BC. After one full cycle, the phases of the moon recur on the same dates – in other words, it's the time you have to wait before your diary will again be correct in its listing of the full moons. The Metonic cycle was responsible for the entry into the language of the word decennoval (or decennovenal) which means of, or pertaining to, a period of nineteen years.

Nineteen is a sacred number in the Baha'i faith, in which the year is divided into nineteen months of nineteen days each. Shakespeare, however, was distinctly less fond of the number nineteen, using it only three times in his entire work, fewer than any other small number.

Nineteen is also the number of:
acres of pizza eaten daily in USA
boxing riots in US 1960-72
cheeses that can be made from 9 gallons of goat's milk according to
    Aristotle
days in the gestation period of a laboratory mouse
grades of pencil from 9H to 9B
grams in the average weight of a Chinese man's testicle
guardians of hell
guns in a salute for the Vice-President of the United States
Hungarian rhapsodies by Liszt
largest ordinal adverb in the *OED* – firstly, secondly, thirdly up to
    nineteenthly are listed, but not twentiethly
percentage of world's goats living in India
percentage of world's pineapples from Thailand
stations on the Baku underground

Finally, we must mention the curious phrase 'nineteen to the dozen' to mean at a very fast rate, though why nineteen is chosen rather than, say, eighteen or twenty is a matter for speculation.

The only known film with '19' in its title is:
Montparnasse 19 (1957): biographical drama on the last weeks of
    Modigliani

'Then come kiss me, sweet and twenty,
Youth's a stuff will not endure.'
William Shakespeare, *Twelfth Night*, 1601

Twenty, as two times ten, plays a significant role in our counting systems, as is seen in the French *quatre-vingts* (four-twenties) to mean eighty and the English 'score' to mean twenty of anything. The latter probably derives from the practice of counting herds of sheep or cattle in twenties, perhaps keeping tally by making a notch or 'score' on a piece of wood. The lifespan allotted to us in the Bible – 'three score years and ten' – and Abraham Lincoln's 'four score and seven years ago' confirm that counting in twenties used to be reasonably widespread. Around the fourth century AD, the Mayans used a counting system with base twenty (properly termed 'vigesimal'). Old German also used to have a word *Schneise* which meant a rope on which twenty codfish were left to dry.

Other words that indicate the number twenty include 'vicenary' (of a group of twenty), 'vicennial' (of a period of twenty years) and anything beginning with the prefix 'icosa-'. The regular icosahedron, for example, has twenty faces, each of which is an equilateral triangle, and icosasenic means lasting the equivalent of time of twenty short syllables. Icosian simply means related to twenty.

Twenty is also the number of:
bottles in a nebuchadnezzar
feet from side to side in a badminton doubles court
hundredweight in a ton
lascivious turtles mentioned in the *Merry Wives of Windsor* ('*Well, I will
    find you twenty lascivious turtles ere one chaste man.*')
major golf championships won by Jack Nicklaus
numbers round the edge of a dart board
pages the Pentagon's Dept of Food Procurement takes to describe hot
    chocolate
points for a minor suit trick in contract bridge
pounds in the record weight of a cucumber
questions in the famous quiz game
relations one couldn't wed after 1949
square feet in area of an average human's skin
tons weight of the average iceberg
Wimbledon titles won by Billie-Jean King
years' marriage for a china anniversary
years Rip van Winkle slept

Films and other works celebrating the number twenty include:

20-Mule Team (1940): adventures of borax miners in the Old West

Love at Twenty (1963): romance directed by Andrzej Wajda and François Truffaut

20 Shades of Pink (1976): worried artist drama with Eli Wallach and Anna Jackson

Twenty Bucks (1993): comedy with Spalding Grey and Christopher Lloyd

Twenty Years After (1845): Alexandre Dumas's sequel to *The Three Musketeers*

Twenty Glances at the Infant Jesus (1944), a piano work by Olivier Messiaen

■ 21

'When I was one-and-twenty
I heard a wise man say
"Give crowns and pounds and guineas
But not your heart away;
Give pearls away and rubies,
But keep your fancy free."
But I was one-and-twenty,
No use to talk to me.'
A. E. Houseman, *A Shropshire Lad*, 1896

Until 1970, in Britain, you had to wait until you were twenty-one to do most of the things you can now do when you are eighteen. An age of majority of twenty-one, however, still remains for certain aspects of life including becoming an MP, taking your seat in the House of Lords, and adopting a child.

Why twenty-one was chosen in the first place as the age of majority remains something of a mystery, though in the light of the mystic connections of the numbers three and seven perhaps their product might be expected to have attained a special significance.

Twenty-one is also the number of:

gallons of beer drunk per capita each year in Australia

guns in a salute for the American President. This practice originated as a royal salute in Britain from ships of the line, which had a maximum of twenty-one guns along one side of the vessel

letters in the language of the angels, according to Elizabethan mystics John Dee and Edward Kelly

---

47 piglets starred in "Babe"

piano concerti by Mozart – although the numbering of such concerti goes well beyond 21, several of the early ones were no more than transcriptions of works by other composers

pips on a die

republics of the Russian Federation

shillings in a guinea

years of the Twenty-One Years' War, from 1701-1721, between Russia and Sweden

Films with twenty-one in their titles include:

Free, Blonde and Twenty-One (1940): comedy romance

Twenty-One Days Together (1940): three weeks in the company of Robert Newton and Laurence Olivier

21 Hours at Munich (1976): TV film drama based on the Arab terrorist murders at the 1972 Olympics

21 Jump Street (1987): Johnny Depp in a high-school crime drama

Twenty-One (1991): comedy romance with Patsy Kensit and Patrick Ryecart

■ 22

'For two-and-twenty sons I never wept,
Because they died in honour's lofty bed.'
William Shakespeare, *Titus Andronicus*, 1594

Twenty-two is a number with deep mystic significance because it has been calculated to be the number of things made by God in the six days of creation: on Day One: unformed matter, angels, light, the upper heavens, earth, water, air; Day Two: the firmament; Day Three: the seas, seeds, grass and trees; Day Four: the sun, moon and stars; Day Five: fish, aquatic reptiles and flying creatures; Day Six: wild beasts, domestic animals, land reptiles and man. That list was first given by Isidor of Seville in the seventh century, and bears all the ingenuity of a man determined to draw up a list with the same number of elements as there are letters in the Hebrew alphabet. So God made the twenty-two things comprising the world, and told man about it in an alphabet of the same number of letters. It is therefore no coincidence that the Revelation of St John the Divine has twenty-two chapters, and St Augustine's *City of God* was written in twenty-two books.

All of which explains why the Tarot pack has twenty-two cards and why occultists refer to the 'Twenty-two paths' of their travels. But it does not explain Joseph Heller's choice of the title *Catch-22* for his most famous novel, particularly in view his decision to change it from *Catch-18* shortly before publication.

Twenty-two also has two meanings beyond the purely numerical. Since twenty-two carat used to be the quality of gold required for coinage, the expression 'twenty-two carat' or simply 'twenty-two' signified a level close to perfection. It could, on the other hand, also mean a rifle, from the .22 calibre bullets it fired.

Twenty-two is also the number of:
balls in snooker
children fathered by Siamese twins Chang and Eng Bunker
chromosomes of a hamster
consonants in the language of the Kiowa Indians of SW America
days in the gestation period of a rat
different colours of undyed llama hair
different meanings of 'fine' listed in the *OED*
dynasties of Chinese emperors
hours a koala sleeps each day on average
percentage of world's beer made in USA, cheese made in USA and wine made in France
square-shaped Hebrew letters – the writing of God
srutis (quarter-tones) in an octave of Indian music
times on average an American opens the fridge each day
yards between wickets in cricket

Twenty-two is a rare visitor to film titles, except for these two:
Twenty Plus Two (1961): detective story with David Janssen
Catch-22 (1970): Alan Arkin in the screen version of Joseph Heller's book

Finally, lets us not forget the findings of T. L. Kinsey, as reported in *Audio-Typing and Electric Typewriters* in 1964:
'*It takes twenty-two times more mechanical energy to operate a manual typewriter than to operate an IBM electric typewriter.*'

And, as Lord Byron put it in his 'Stanza Written on the Road Between Florence and Pisa':
'*The myrtle and ivy of sweet two-and-twenty*
Are worth all your laurels, though ever so plenty.'

'She was married, charming, chaste and twenty-three.'
Lord Byron, *Don Juan*, 1819-24

Twenty-three is the smallest number of people you have to have in a room for there to be a greater than even chance that two of them have the same birthday. (Forgetting the awkward case of anyone born on 29 February, which adds a messy complication to the calculation: the second person has 364 chances out of 365 of having a different birthday from the first, the third has 363 chances out of 365 of avoiding the birthdays of the first two, the fourth has 362 out of 365 chances of differing from the other three, and if you multiply 364/365×363/365×362/365×361/365, and so on, the answer drops below 0.5 when the twenty-second term is reached.) That fact, however, has nothing to do with the expression 'twenty-three skidoo', meaning scram, which first appeared in the United States in the early years of the twentieth century: nobody knows where it came from. The 'skidoo' probably owes something to the older 'skedaddle' (or simply skids), but why the 'twenty-three' became attached is a mystery. This explanation, from J. F. Kelly's *Man With Grip* (1906) seems as likely as any: *'I can see a reason for "skidoo," said one, 'and for "23" also. Skidoo from skids and "23" from 23rd Street that has ferries and depots for 80 per cent of the railroads leaving New York.'*

Twenty-three is also the number of:
camels once offered by an Arab for the actress Diana Dors
centimetres in a breadth – a measurement in flag-making dating from a
    time when flag cloth was made in 23 cm strips
hours a week spent on household chores by the average British father
letters in the longest place name in the US: Nunathloogagamintbingoi
    Dunes, Alaska
meteorites known to have fallen on the UK
minutes taken for an eighteen-month old girl to toddle the length of Pall
    Mall on 11 May 1749 winning several bets by seven minutes
people on a grand jury
percentage of world's tangerines from Japan, watermelons from China,
    and TV receivers made in China
ratio of land dug up in the US for resource exploitation to that filled with
    garbage
tenses in the Santali language of India
towns and cities in the US called Moscow
tons of strawberries eaten at Wimbledon in 1990
years Yorick's skull was buried before Hamlet came across it. ('This skull

hath lain I' th' earth three-and-twenty years.')

In films, and other works, twenty-three is memorable for:
Pier 23 (1951): detective suspense
23 Paces to Baker Street (1956): Van Johnson is a blind writer who foils a
    kidnapping
Poem: 'On His Being Arrived at the Age of Twenty-Three' by John
    Milton. ('How soon hath Time, the subtle thief of youth, Stolen on
    his wing my three and twentieth year . . .')

■ 24

*'This is the kind of Babylonish lexicography of Johnson's Dictionary,
which gives twenty-four meanings, or shadows of meaning, to the word
"from".'*
J. Gilchrist, 1816

Twenty-four is a number of great significance in the Jain religion and in
the Isle of Man. In the latter, it is the number of members of the
legislative assembly the 'House of Keys' which, from 1585-1734, was
officially termed 'The Twenty-four Keys'. In the Manx language, it is
commonly referred to as *'Yn Kiare as Feed'* (the four and twenty).
   The Jain religion is said to have had 24 founding prophets, the *Jinas,*
also known as *Tirthankara,* who can be distinguished from each other
only by their colour, stature and longevity. Two are red, two white, two
blue, two black and sixteen golden, or yellowish-brown. On the other
criteria, they vary from *Rishaba,* the first *Jina,* who was 500 poles tall
and lived 8,400,000 great years, to *Jahávina,* the last of *Jina,* who was the
size of an ordinary man and lived on earth for only forty years.
   Mathematically, a fluoroid is a solid bounded by twenty-four
triangular planes which plays an important role in crystallography. This
figure ought not to be confused with the icositetrahedron, a figure
bounded by twenty-four equal and similar trapezia, nor the
tetrahexahedron, which also has twenty-four faces.

Twenty-four is also the number of:
blackbirds baked in a pie
carats in pure gold
dollars paid to the American Indians for Manhattan Island
draughtsmen in a set
grains in a pennyweight
hours in a day
letters in the Greek alphabet
letters in the Korean alphabet

points on a backgammon board
recorded accidents in the UK in 1994 involving toilet rolls
ribs of a human (7 true pairs, 5 'false' pairs)
scruples in a Troy ounce
string quartets by Mozart
syllables in a sijo – a Korean lyric poem of three lines

In film titles, the number '24' is nearly always followed by the word
'Hours', as the following list shows:
24 Hours (1931): Regis Toomey murders Miriam Hopkins, but Clive
  Brook is convicted (based on the novel by Louis Bromfield)
24 Hours in a Woman's Life (1961): widow Ingrid Bergman falls in love
  with a gambler
24 Hours to Kill (1966): Mickey Rooney crime caper
24 Hours in a Woman's Life (1968): romance drama based on a story by
  Stefan Zweig
24 Hours to Midnight (1992): martial arts gangster story

Literature: *The Twenty-Four Days Before Christmas* (1964) by the
  American children's author Madeleine L'Engle

■ 25

'Touchstone: How old are you, friend?
William: Five and twenty, sir.
Touchstone: A ripe age.'
William Shakespeare, *As You Like It*, 1600

Twenty-five, said Beverley Nichols in his book *Twenty-Five*, is the ideal
age at which to write your autobiography. It is, of course, also the square
of the hypotenuse in the smallest Pythagorean triangle with sides of
integer length. It is also the only square that is two less than a cube:
$25 = 5^2 = 3^3 - 2$.
   Dylan Thomas chose this number for his collection called *Twenty-Five
Poems*, and there is a 25-yard line in hockey and formerly on a rugby
pitch. In Cockney slang, twenty-five pounds is called a pony, though
nobody knows why. Two ponies, of course, make a monkey (→fifty).

Twenty-five is also the number of:
appearances by Richard Cohen in the British Sabre championships finals
  in consecutive years, the record figure for any publisher of a Book of
  Numbers
beats per minute of elephant heart

gallons of soft drink drunk per capita each year in Australia
helicopter pads in Antarctica
languages in which Monopoly is available
minutes it takes the average Briton to get to work
moles on average adult body
miles per hour of the speed limit in Britain in 1903
percentage of world's asses in China

seconds per Japanese baby born in 1994
years' marriage for a silver anniversary

Films with '25' in the title include:
25, Firemen's Street (1973): drama of wartime upheaval in Budapest
The 25th Hour (1967): World War II drama comedy

■ 26

*'It was not long after that that everybody was 26. During the next two
or three years all the young men were 26 years old. It was the right age
apparently for that time and place.'*
Gertrude Stein, *The Autobiography of Alice B. Toklas*

Twenty-six is the number of letters of the alphabet and the Counties of
Ireland that formed the Irish Free State in 1921: Galway, Leitrim, Mayo,
Roscommon, Sligo, Carlow, Dublin, Kildare, Kilkenny, Laoighis,
Longford, Louth, Meath, Offaly, Westmeath, Wexford, Wicklow, Clare,
Cork, Kerry, Limerick, Tipperary, Cavan, Donegal, Monaghan.

Twenty-six is also the number of:

black or red cards in a pack

chromosomes of a frog

French people expelled from Britain between 1907 and 1914 for
    prostitution and procuring

New Zealand's Test Match score against England 1954-55, the lowest
    ever by a Test side

percentage of world's strawberries grown in the US

popes to have been assassinated

self-governing states of India

species of goat

CAPRA.   Plate CXXI.

Chamois Goat.   African Goat.
                  Female.   Male.

Syrian Goat.
    Female.   Male.   Wild Goat

                Common Goat.
    Male.   Female.

thickness of walls of Babylon in metres

times Mount Mayon, a volcano on Luzon in the Philippines, erupted on 24 March 1993

vertebrae in the human body

ways Giles Rose, chef to Charles II, could fold table napkins

Twenty-six is also where the numbers stop in the *OED*: 'One' to 'twenty-five' are all given with meanings of their own, but twenty-six is listed as a headword only in the phrase 'Twenty-six Counties'.

Twenty-six does, however, appear in the title of one film, one book and one revolutionary movement:

26 Men (1958): a made-for-TV western; *Twenty-Six Men and a Girl*, by Maxim Gorky; and the 'Twenty-sixth of July Movement', Fidel Castro's group of Cubans that overthrew the dictator Fulgencio Batista in 1959.

■ 27

'Volumnia: He had before this last expedition twenty-five wounds upon him.
Menenius: Now it's twenty-seven; every gash was an enemy's grave.'
William Shakespeare, *Coriolanus*, 1607

Twenty-seven, apart from being the cube of three, has a number of fine mathematical properties. First it has been proved that every integer is the sum of at most twenty-seven prime numbers. Second, if you take any three-digit multiple of twenty-seven and move the last digit to the front, or the front digit to the end, than the new number formed will also be divisible by twenty-seven. For example: 783 = 27×29, 837 = 27×31, 378 = 27×14.

Finally, there is a game with numbers called the 'Syracuse algorithm': start with any number; if it is even, halve it; if it is odd, multiply it by three and add one. Then repeat the process with the answer. If you proceed in this fashion it is believed (but has never been proven) that whatever number you start with you will always eventually get to the cycle, 4, 2, 1, 4, 2, 1 . . . The number 27, however, gives you one of the longest runs of all small numbers, starting 27, 82, 41, 124, 62, 31, 94, 47 . . . and peaking at 9,232 before eventually reaching 4, 2, 1 after 111 steps.

Twenty-seven is also the number of:

amendments to the US constitution

charges against the king in the US Declaration of Independence

cubic feet in a cubic yard
miles per hour in the maximum speed of a human runner
plastic bottles needed to make enough PVC yarn for a jumper
players a side in the sixteenth-century Italian game of Calcio – an early
    form of football. Players had to be gentlemen, aged 18-45, beautiful
    and vigorous, of gallant bearing and good report
words for snow in Inuit

Two films have twenty-seven in the title:
The 27th Day (1957): aliens give earthmen capsules that can destroy the
    world
27a (1974): Australian drama

And one play:
Twenty-Seven Wagons Full of Cotton by Tennessee Williams

■ 28

'Mr Clarke packed all his furs on 28 horses.'
Washington Irving, *Astoria*, 1849

Twenty-eight centimetres per second is the top speed of a lone lobster.
However, a line of lobsters, each
clinging to the tail of the one in
front, have been observed moving at
speeds of up to thirty-five
centimetres per second as they walk
along the sea bed. The kinetics of
such lobster migration queues have
attracted some research, including
one famous experiment in which
lobster carcasses were tied together
with metallic wire and dragged, by a
weight and pulley apparatus, along
the bottom of a tank. The
experiments proved that lobsters
reduce water resistance by linking in
a line. Observers of migrating
lobsters have also noticed that the
front lobster in a queue will
periodically stand aside, let the others
pass, then join in again at the back,
just as in a cycle pursuit team.

Lobsters apart, twenty-eight is an important number in Islam, with the link between the twenty-eight mansions of the moon in astrology and the twenty-eight letters of the Arabic alphabet seen as highly significant by some mediaeval theologians. Since the Koran also mentions exactly twenty-eight Prophets before Muhammad, it ties together beautifully. The twenty-eight Arabic letters were also used as the basis for a counting system with the first nine letters used as the numbers 1 to 9, the next nine letters representing the tens, from 10 to 90, and the next nine the hundreds from 100 to 900. The final letter represented 1,000. Much earlier, a similar counting system was used in the Egyptian *Thousand Songs of Thebes* written around 1300 BC which comprises just twenty-eight poems.

Mathematically, 28 is a perfect number, being equal to the sum of its divisors: 28 = 1+2+4+7+14.

Twenty-eight is also the number of:
countries that sold arms to both sides in Iran–Iraq war, 1980-88
days in February
days it takes our outer layer of skin to be totally replaced
digits in a cubit in ancient Egypt: a digit was the width of a finger, a
    cubit was the length from elbow to fingertip
hours a week the average American spends watching television
inches height of cricket wicket
inches length of the common or true civet (according to Hulme, 1862)
inches length of the Congo snake (according to Tenney, 1865)
letters in Phoenician alphabet
people per square kilometre in the US
percentage of the world's tea from India
points on the Beaume scale of saccharinity
pounds record weight of a radish
pounds weight of carbon in the average human body
properties for sale on a Monopoly board
weeks 'Don't be Cruel' was in the US charts in 1956. The B-side was
    'Hound Dog'. The singer was Elvis Presley

And let us not forget the Twenty-eight Parakeet – a yellow-collared parakeet of Australia whose cry sounds like 'twenty-eight'.

The only film is:
The Unbeaten 28 (1981): American-made kung fu violence

'Nine-and-twenty-knights of fame
Hung their shields in Branksome Hall;
Nine-and-twenty squires of name
Brought them their steeds to bower from stall;
Nine-and-twenty yeomen tall
Waited duteous on them all:
They were all knights of mettle true,
Kinsmen to the bold Buccleuch.'
Walter Scott, *The Lay of the Last Minstrel,* 1805

For a prime number, 29 is unexceptional, except perhaps for the fact that $2n^2+29$ is prime for all values of n from 1 to 28. Even that, however, is not as interesting as the 'Song of Twenty-Nine' by Oliver Wendell Holmes, which contains the couplet: 'At last the day is ended, The tutor screws no more'. (Screw meaning to examine in great detail.)

Twenty-nine is also the number of:
adults living in the islands of St Kilda – none of whom bothered to get
    their names on the electoral register for the 1997 British general
    election (twenty-two ran a missile-tracking station, six studied sheep,
    one was warden of a bird sanctuary)
bones in the skull (though some sources
    prefer the figure of 22, which excludes
    the ears and the hyoid bone,
    between jaw and larynx)

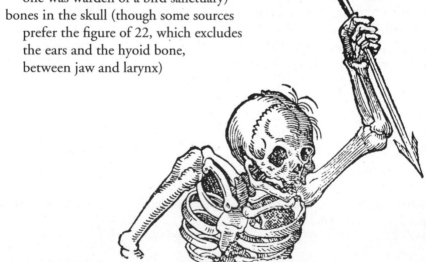

days in leap February
degrees of angle of arc permitted for a javelin throw
feet of intestine in a human body
hours it took to get from New York to Chicago in 1873

letters in floccipaucinihilipilification, the action of estimating as
   worthless; a word used by both Walter Scott and Robert Southey
provinces of the Byzantine empire
racial groups of man according to Joseph Deniker (1900) and Egon von
   Eickstedt (1934), though their classification systems differed
symbols in Palantyne, a mechanical shorthand invented in 1940
the track for the Chattanooga Choo-Choo in the 1941 song by Mack
   Gordon (music by Harry Warren)

Twenty-nine also crops up in the titles of the following films:
Track 29 (1988): Christoper Lloyd in a violent comedy
29th Street (1991): lottery-winner meets mobsters in comedy-drama
   based on true story

■ **30**

'Some thirty inches from my nose
The frontier of my Person goes.'
W. H. Auden, *Prologue: the Birth of Architecture*, 1966

Thirty is traditionally the age most women lie about. 'The best ten years
of a woman's life are between twenty-nine and thirty' went the old
saying. Indeed, a recent informal survey of the stated ages of successful
women confirmed that considerably more of them were twenty-nine
than might reasonably have been expected. Yet Honoré de Balzac knew
the truth. In his novel *The Woman of Thirty*, he wrote in 1832: 'For a
young man, a woman of thirty has irresistible attractions.'

Thirty is also the number of:
bones in an arm, including the hand (though some authorities say there
   are thirty-two)
cheeses that can be made from nine gallons of cow's milk, according to
   Aristotle
classic races won by Lester Piggott
days that September, April, June and November hath (from a rhyme by
   William Harrison, written in 1577)
edges on a dodecahedron or icosahedron
fatal accidents on British airlines since 1950
goals scored for Scotland by both Kenny Dalglish and Denis Law
magistrates – the Thirty Tyrants – imposed by Sparta over Athens at the
   end of the Peloponnesian War in 404 BC
pieces of silver given to Judas
points for trick in spades, hearts or no-trumps (after the first) in bridge
relations one could not marry before 1949

59 square miles of British Virgins

STONEHENGE in its original state.

STONEHENGE i

upright stones originally in the Sarsen circle at Stonehenge (of which
    sixteen are still standing)
variations in Bach's Goldberg Variations
years of age an ancient Roman had to have attained to become a tribune
years' marriage for a pearl anniversary

Films and other works with thirty in their titles include:
Thirty-Day Princess (1934): comedy with Cary Grant
Thirty Seconds Over Tokyo (1944): Van Johnson bombs the Japs
30 (1959): a drama set in Los Angeles

STONEHENGE in its Present state.

...resent state.

The 30-Foot Bride of Candy Rock (1959): sci-fi comedy – Lou Costello's last film, and his only one without Bud Abbott

30 Years of Fun (1963): silent movie comedy compilation

30 Winchester for El Diablo (1965): western

30 is a Dangerous Age, Cynthia (1968): Dudley Moore as a pianist seeking fame before he is thirty

Hurry Up or I'll be Thirty (1973): Danny de Vito comedy

Thirty Tales by H. E. Bates

Thirty Years a Detective (1884), an autobiographical reminiscence by Allan Pinkerton

'Toad that under cold stone
Days and nights hast thirty-one
Sweltered venom sleeping got,
Boil thou first i' the charmèd pot.'
William Shakespeare, *Macbeth*, 1606

Thirty-one is the number of days in most of our months, though the reasons date back two thousand years for their lurching between thirty and thirty-one, with February lagging behind, even in a leap year. The word 'month' has the same root as 'moon', and it means the time between one new moon and the next. Which, if adhered to strictly, would give an average of about twenty-nine-and-a-half days. The trouble, as usual with anything to do with the calendar, is that the times of the relative orbits of the earth round the sun (a year), the moon round the earth (a month), and the earth about its axis (a day) are not integral multiples of one another. The Romans began with ten months: Martius (of the god Mars), Aprilis (derivation obscure), Maius (goddess Maia), Junius (goddess Juno), Quinctilis (fifth), Sextilis (sixth), September (seventh), October (eighth), November (ninth) and December (tenth). Then Januarius (Janus) and Februarius (of Februa, the feast of purification) were added, and the fifth and sixth months were renamed after Julius and Augustus Caesar. March, May, July and October had thirty-one days, February had twenty-eight, and the rest had twenty-nine, which added up to 355 days, some ten days short of a full year. An extra month called Mercedonius was therefore added in alternate years, beginning after 22 February, and going on for twenty-two or twenty-three days before February was resumed. The result was a four-year cycle, of 355, 377, 355 and 378 days. Or it would have been if the priests had not occasionally neglected to put in the extra month.

In 46 BC, the calendar was ninety days out, so Julius Caesar asked the mathematician Sosigenes to take a hand. The result was the Julian calendar, which came into force in 45 BC. First, however, Julius Caesar had to resolve the problems of 46 BC, which afterwards became known as the 'year of confusion'. By the time it was over, 46 BC had had 445 days – the usual 355, plus a Mercedonius of twenty-three and an extra sixty-seven days, to give the sun a chance to catch up, inserted between November and December. For the rest of the story, →365.

Thirty-one is also the number of:
bones in human leg

children of Orihah in the Book of Mormon
counties in the US named after George Washington
days in January, March, May, July, August, October, December
days in the gestation period of a rabbit
Grand Prix wins by Nigel Mansell
letters in the Cyrillic alphabet
marriages in Sweden in 1990 between female doctors and male nurses
    (→2,396)
mean February temperature in Denmark in degrees Fahrenheit
miles length of the Channel tunnel
people who died (in the short-term) from radiation sickness or burns
    after the accident at Chernobyl in 1986
points the played cards may not exceed in a hand of cribbage
states in Mexico
syllables in a Tanka, an ancient Japanese verse form once restricted to the
    imperial family
years Josiah reigned in Jerusalem (Second Book of Kings)

Thirty-one is very rare in film titles, with the exception of:
Adalen 31 (1969): Swedish romance directed by Bo Widerberg

'Thirty-one' is also the name of a card game in which the object is to
attain a score of exactly thirty-one points – which explains the quotation
that begins our next number.

■ **32**

'Well, was it fit for a servant to use his master so;
being, for aught I could see, two and thirty, a pip out?'
William Shakespeare, *The Taming of the Shrew*, 1594

Thirty-two is the fifth power of two and therefore the number of leaves
of paper you end up with if you fold a single sheet in half five times, then
cut the edges. This explains why the English language is blessed with a
word as ugly as thirtytwomo (also written as 32mo or XXXIImo) – the
size of a book made of sheets folded in such a fashion.

   As the fifth power of two, thirty-two is also the number of subsets that
can be formed from five objects. In other words, it is the number of
different ways in which you can hold up the fingers of one hand.

   Thirty-two is also the number of teeth in a full human set, which is
why Horace Fletcher, in his *ABC of Nutrition* (1903), recommended you
should chew each mouthful of food precisely thirty-two times. William
Gladstone followed this advice, though the *Practitioner*, in June 1907,

scornfully commented: 'The Fletcherites, who, so far from not giving two bites to a cherry, insist on thirty-two to a mashed potato.'

Thirty-two is also the number of:
clues in the world's first crossword (which appeared in *New York World* on 21 December 1913)
days in office of William Harrison, the shortest-serving US President
demi-semiquavers in a semibreve, which is why the Americans, who call the semibreve a 'whole note', refer to the demi-semiquaver as a 'thirty-second note'
directions on a compass
Fahrenheit degrees for the freezing point of water
inches of mercury in normal barometric pressure
letters in the modern Russian Cyrillic alphabet
pints' capacity of a pig's stomach

Thirty-two is the smallest number not to have occurred in a film title.

■ 33

'When think you that the sword goes up again?
Never, till Caesar's three and thirty wounds
Be well avenged.'
William Shakespeare, *Julius Caesar*, 1599

'Thirty-three' was the term once used for a long-playing gramophone record, though its rate of rotation was actually thirty-three and a third revolutions per minute. First announced in 1948, and introduced in 1951, the 'long-playing' records could contain twenty minutes of music, compared with just over four minutes on the old seventy-eight rpm records. The amount of music possible on one record doubled again in 1956, when 'fine-groove' recording equipment was introduced. Then compact discs arrived, and we threw all our gramophone records, 33s, 45s and 78s, away. Anyone born in '33, it should be noted, will have been 45 in '78.

Thirty-three also plays a strong tune in Judaeo-Christian tradition, with King David reigning for thirty-three years and Jesus Christ living on earth for thirty-three years.

Thirty-three is also the number of:

cantos favoured by Dante in the Divine Comedy

counties in Scotland until 1975, when the counties were abolished and amalgamated into nine administrative regions, which were in turn, replaced in 1996 by thirty-two unitary authorities

days' record for going round the world by car

Diabelli variations by Beethoven

films made by Elvis Presley

French expelled from Great Britain 1907-14 for brothel-keeping

'The Immortal Thirty-three', a group of Uruguayan patriots who, in 1825, revolted against Brazilian rule, leading eventually to the establishment of Uruguay as an independent republic in 1830

inches height of hurdles in women's 100m

islands in Kiribati

life expectancy in Britain in the Middle Ages

percentage of world's coconuts grown in India

species of parrot in the world

species of Terrapin listed in the Catalogue of Animals at the London Zoological Gardens in 1896

terms of abuse for tax collectors listed in the *Onomasticon* of the Greek grammarian Julius Pollux (180-238)

warships in Napoleon's fleet at the Battle of Trafalgar, which were destroyed by the twenty-seven ships under Nelson's command.

Thirty-three is a better number for film titles than its two predecessors, having appeared in:

Case 33: Antwerp (1965): spy story

Naked Gun 33⅓: The Final Insult (1994); cop spoof with Leslie Nielsen

Literature includes: *Thirty and Three* (1954), a collection of essays by the Canadian author Hugh MacLennan.

'Stella this day is thirty-four
(We shan't dispute a year or more.)'
Jonathan Swift, *Stella's Birthday Works*, 1718-19

Thirty-four is an interesting number in the study of thermometers, for it is the average Celsius temperature at the hottest place on earth, which is Dallol, Ethiopia, as measured between 1960 and 1966. It is also the average Celsius temperature of the hedgehog, which sounds potentially very uncomfortable for Ethiopian hedgehogs.

Thirty-four is also the number of:
consonants in the Siamese language (to go with its twelve vowels),
    according to the traveller H. Malcom writing in 1840
miles that must be walked to get rid of 1 pound of fat
percentage of the world's olive oil from Italy, oranges from Brazil and
    gold mined in South Africa
Test-match centuries of Sunil Gavaskar
years' age of the oldest cat on record

THERMOMETER.   Plate DVII.

'No person except a natural-born citizen, or a citizen of the United States, at the time of the adoption of this Constitution, shall be eligible to the office of President; neither shall any person be eligible to that office who shall not have attained to the age of thirty-five years, and been fourteen years a resident within the United States.'
US Constitution

Thirty-five is an infuriating number for makers of mathematical games and puzzles. It is the number of distinct hexominoes – shapes formed from six squares joined by their edges – and the total area of those thirty-five shapes is therefore 6×35, which is 210. Yet although 210 is the area of a variety of rectangles (3×70, or 5×42, or 6×35, or 7×30, or 10×21, or 14×15) which might plausibly be filled with the hexominoes, there is, in fact, no way of putting the thirty-five shapes together to form any of them.

Thirty-five is also the number of:
articles of clothing bought by the average American male each year
blends of tea in the average teabag
cubic feet of gas a cow belches each day
days in the gestation period of a hedgehog
days on which Easter may fall (according to a parliamentary act in the
   reign of George II, Easter falls on the first Sunday after the full moon
   which happens on, or next after, 21 March. In 1928 the House of
   Commons agreed to fix Easter in the week 9-15 April, subject to
   satisfactory consultations among the various Christian churches.
   Those consultations have yet to be concluded.)
dots on a computer screen needed for all the letters of the alphabet
   (→576)
feet in length of the longest reticulated python
fox ranches in Alaska in 1900
gallons of water a camel can drink in 10 minutes
metres length of a standard toilet roll
muscles used to move the human hand
Russians and Poles expelled from Great Britain 1907-14 for brothel-
   keeping
seconds it took an enormous angry rhinoceros to eat up James Henry
   Trotter's parents in Roald Dahl's *James and the Giant Peach*
tribes of the Roman people, from whom a body of judges, three from
   each tribe, was appointed to decide civil disputes. For the sake of

linguistic simplicity, this body of 105 men was called the *centumvir* (hundred men)

years' marriage for a coral anniversary

Books: *Thirty-Five Years of a Dramatic Author's Life*, (1859) by E. Fitzball
Thirty-Five Poems (1940) by Sir Herbert Read
Tall, Balding, Thirty-Five (1966) by Anthony Firth

■ 36

'A courtmartial sat upon him, and he was asked which he liked better, to run the gauntlet six and thirty times through the whole regiment, or to have his brains blown out with a dozen musket balls?'
Voltaire, *Candide*, 1759

The first Chinese Empire, or so the legend goes, was divided into thirty-six provinces and surrounded by thirty-six foreign peoples. As a square of the first perfect number, six, thirty-six is the sort of number to crop up in legend and mysticism. So perhaps it is no surprise that the three aspects of each of the twelve zodiac signs give a total of thirty-six.

Thirty-six is the number of Stratagems of Shanshiliu Ji, a Chinese philosopher who flourished sometime before AD 500. They are as follows:

STRATAGEMS WHEN WINNING
1 Crossing the sea by treachery
2 Besiege Wei to rescue Zhao
3 Murder with a borrowed knife
4 Let the enemy make the first move
5 Loot a burning house
6 Feint to the east, attack to the west.

STRATAGEMS FOR CONFRONTING THE ENEMY
7 Make something out of nothing
8 Secretly cross at Chencang
9 Watch the fire from the opposite shore
10 Hide a dagger with a smile
11 Lead away a goat in passing
12 Sacrifice plums for peaches

STRATAGEMS FOR ATTACK
13 Beat the grass to startle the snake

14 Reincarnation
15 Lure the tiger out of the mountains
16 Allow the enemy some latitude so you can finish him off later
17 Throw out a brick to attract Jade
18 To catch bandits capture their leader

STRATAGEMS FOR CHAOTIC SITUATIONS
19 Pull the firewood from under the cauldron
20 Fishing in troubled waters
21 The cicada sheds its skin
22 Close the door to capture the thief
23 Make friends with distant countries and attack your neighbour
24 Borrow a road to send an expedition against Guo

STRATAGEMS FOR GAINING GROUND
25 Replace the beams and pillars with rotten timber
26 Point at the mulberry to curse the locust tree
27 Play the fool
28 Remove the ladder after the enemy goes upstairs
29 Put fake blossoms on the tree
30 The guest plays the host

STRATAGEMS WHEN LOSING
31 The beauty trap
32 The empty fort ploy
33 Counter-espionage
34 The self-injury ploy
35 Interlocking stratagems
36 Sometimes retreat is the best option

Thirty-six is also the number of:
feet width of a tennis court (doubles)
grams of buns, scones and teacakes eaten by the average Briton each week
grams of butter eaten by the average Briton each week
inches height of hurdles in men's 400m
inches in a yard
miles travelled each year by taxi by the average Briton
years' life expectancy at birth in Malawi and Zambia, the world's lowest

In the cinema, thirty-six is celebrated by the following films:
36 Hours (1965): World War II suspense
36 Hours to Hell (1977): World War II epic
36 Fillette (1988): sexual awakening of 14-year-old French girl – the title
   is a well-known dress size

"Women should marry when they are about eighteen years of age, and men at seven and thirty.'
Aristotle, *Politics, c.* 330 BC

Thirty-seven is a significant number in the history of flying. It was the length in metres of the first flight made by Orville Wright on 17 December 1903, and was also the number of minutes it took Louis Bleriot, on 25 July 1909, to become the first person to fly across the English Channel.

Thirty-seven is also the number of:
comets discovered by Jean-Louis Pons (1761-1831)
degrees Celsius in normal human body temperature
grams of protein needed each day by a man of average weight
metres per minute at which escalators in underground stations and
    airports travel. Those in shops tend to go at the slower speed of 27
    metres per minute.
plays of Shakespeare
US states with the death penalty
universities in Australia
volumes in the encyclopaedia of natural history compiled by Pliny
    the Elder

■ 38

'Give me a thirty-eight every time. Just flick back the hammer and let her go. I'll drop anyone at five hundred feet.'
William Burroughs, *Junkie*, 1953

Thirty-eight is a number associated with danger. Quite apart from being the calibre of a .38 automatic, it is the number of people in the United Kingdom who died of Creutzfeldt-Jacob Disease in 1995 and the number of recorded accidents in homes in the UK in 1994 involving Christmas trees.

Thirty-eight is also the number of:
aeroplanes on show at the world's first great aviation meeting near
    Rheims, France, in 1909
bathrooms in the house that Mike Tyson put up for sale in 1997
chromosomes of a cat

inches in the maximum length of a cricket bat

miles a year cycled by the average Briton

minutes' length of the war in 1896 between Britain and Zanzibar

percentage of Canadian women who prefer chocolate to sex, according to a survey in 1996

professional teams in the Scottish Football League

streets named 'Vostochnaya' (eastern) in the Ukrainian city of Kherson in 1995, when a special renaming committee was established to ease the confusion

times the England football manager Graham Taylor said 'fuck' in one TV documentary

Film: *38: Vienna Before the Fall* (1988): cross-cultural romance under the Nazis

■ 39

'Then I gave not over opening place after place until nine and thirty days were passed, and in that time I had entered every chamber except that one whose door the Princesses had charged me not to open.'
Sir Richard Burton, *Tales from the Arabian Nights*, 1888

The main significance of thirty-nine is that it is one less than forty, but forty, as we shall see, is a number of such great importance that being one less than it is quite an honour. If forty is the upper limit ascribed to

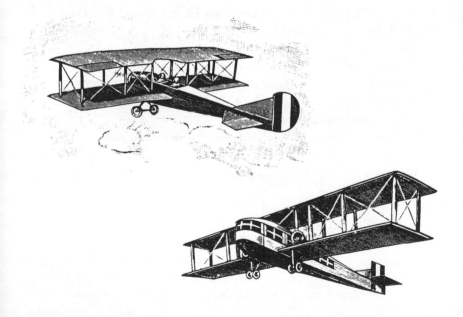

something, then thirty-nine is as far as you are allowed to go. So when forty lashes was considered the greatest permissible punishment, the Law of Moses prescribed a maximum of thirty-nine. St Paul, in his letter to the Corinthians, refers to himself receiving 'forty blows less one'. At about the same there was drawn up a list of the thirty-nine principal types of task that were forbidden on the Jewish sabbath. Later another list was added of thirty-nine further minor things to be avoided. In both cases, the lists gave the impression of leaving one place free, to suggest that the list was not quite all-embracing.

Thirty-nine is also the number of:
Articles of the Church of England, set out in 1563 and approved by
    Parliament in 1571 to settle religious disputes after the Reformation
grammes of tea consumed by the average Briton each week
handkerchiefs used to mop the brow of George IV during his coronation
    in 1821
hockey riots in the US, 1960-72
inches height of hurdles in men's 110 metres
feet in the length of a badminton singles court
people killed by stray bullets in NY city in 1989
people shot dead in gun-related crimes in Japan in 1994
percentage of world's raspberries in 1991 that came from the USSR
Russians and Poles expelled from Great Britain 1907-14 for soliciting
    and importuning
years reign of Henry VI

But for John Buchan, we might never have seen '39' in a film title:
The 39 Steps (1935): Robert Donat as Richard Hannay in Hitchcock's
    classic version of the John Buchan novel. Despite the general
    brilliance of the film, it almost omitted to mention the thirty-nine
    steps of the title, an explanation only being included close to the end
The 39 Steps (1960): Kenneth Moore plays Hannay in the least of the
    screen versions of the book
The 39 Steps (1979): with Robert Powell and Sir John Mills

■ 40

'Nobody loves a fairy when she's forty.'
Arthur W. D. Henley, song title, 1934

Forty, apart from being the only number-word in the English language that has its letters in alphabetical order, is a number with deep Biblical significance. Particularly in the Old Testament, whenever a number is needed that is full of weight and portent, forty seems to be the natural choice. There were the forty days and forty nights during which rain fell during the Flood, then another forty days passed before Noah opened the window of the ark; Moses spent forty days on the mount; Elijah was fed for forty days in the wilderness by ravens; Nineveh was given forty days by Jonah to repent. In the New Testament, Jesus fasted for forty days, and he was seen forty days after his resurrection. Following this tradition, forty days became enshrined in law whenever a suitable period of waiting was required; hence the forty days of quarantine (from the French for 'forty') and the forty days, after the prorogation of the House of Commons, that an MP used to be free from the danger of arrest.

Forty is also the number of:
atoms in a molecule of penicillin
chromosomes of a mouse
days a widow was allowed, under old English law, to remain in her
    husband's house after his death
days allowed in old English law to pay a fine for manslaughter
days in the gestation period of a polecat
days of rain that will follow, proverbially, if it rains on St Swithin's Day;
    weather statistics, however, do not bear this out
the 'Forty Immortals', the members of the French Academy who, once
    elected, are members for life
murders in Belgrade in the first four months of 1997
points for the first no-trump trick in a bridge contract
qualification age in order to be fortified by Phyllosan
thieves encountered by Ali Baba

winks for a short nap
years' marriage for a ruby anniversary
years of Israel in wilderness
Years On, for the Harrow school song

73 letters in the Cambodian alphabet

Films with '40' include:
40 Pounds of Trouble (1963): Stubby Kaye, Tony Curtis, Phil Silvers and a mischievous child
40 Guns to Apache Pass (1967): western with Audie Murphy
40 Graves for 40 Guns (1971): American outlaws steal Mexican relic

■ 41

'Lizzie Borden took an axe
And gave her mother forty whacks;
When she saw what she had done
She gave her father forty-one.'
Anonymous, after the trial of Lizzie Borden in America in 1893

Never trust a homicidal daughter with an axe, or an encyclopaedia that tells you that Mozart wrote forty-one symphonies. Everyone knows, of course, that Mozart's last symphony, number 41 in C major, is the Jupiter, but some of those numbered 1 to 40 were later discovered probably not to have been written by Mozart at all, others are not symphonies but concert overtures, while several of his other compositions deserve the designation of 'symphony' although they are not known as such.

The last Symphony, incidentally, was not known as the Jupiter until some sixty years after Mozart's death. The name was bestowed upon it by Johann Baptist Cramer (1771-1858), a composer and music publisher, who thought it deserved a name that reflected its grandeur. In Germany, they call it the *Synphonie mit der Schlussfuge* (symphony with the final fugue), which is also incorrect, since the final movement, while containing some intricate counterpoint, is not, strictly speaking, a fugue.

Lizzie Borden, by the way, was acquitted of the charge of murdering her parents. All of which adds up to forty-one being one of the most consistently wrong numbers in history.

Forty-one is also the number of:
grams of margarine eaten by the average Briton each week
members on the Venetian council, known as the forty-one, by whom the Doge was elected
pounds in royalties earned by Freud for his book *The Interpretation of Dreams*
riding clubs in Iceland in 1978
years in the longest recorded lifespan of a goldfish

'And in this borrowed likeness of shrunk death
Thou shalt continue two-and-forty hours,
And then awake as from a pleasant sleep.'
William Shakespeare, *Romeo and Juliet*

Forty-two is, as all fans of Douglas Adams's *Hitch-hiker's Guide to the Galaxy* know, the answer to Life, the Universe and Everything. The curious thing, however, is that while Douglas Adams claims to have chosen the number for no particular reason, forty-two also crops up in several ancient religions as a number of great significance. In ancient Egypt, the fate of the dead was supposed to be decided by forty-two demons, each representing one diocese of the country and ready to seize the soul of any individual who had committed a sin within its area of responsibility.

'I know thee, I know thy name, I know the names of the Forty-two Gods who live with thee in this Hall of Maati, who live by keeping ward over sinners, and who feed upon their blood on the day when the consciences of men are reckoned up in the presence of the god Un-Nefer.'

Egyptian *Book of the Dead.*

There was a forty-two-armed Hindu god and forty-two was a sacred number in Tibet. In Judaeo-Christian tradition also, the number forty-two crops up more often than it ought. There were forty-two generations from Abraham to Jesus Christ, forty-two Levitical cities, forty-two boys torn to pieces by bears because they had ridiculed the prophet Elisha (2nd Book of Kings), forty-two sacrifices of Balach in the Book of Numbers and 'forty and two months' which the Gentiles would tread the Holy City, as predicted in the Book of Revelation. (Incidentally, forty-two months is three-and-a-half years, and if you multiply 3½ by 42, you get 147, which is the mystical number of the snooker table.)

Another writer who took a fancy to the number forty-two was Lewis Carroll, but in his case the choice was probably more deliberate. Carroll, in real life the Rev Charles Lutwidge Dodgson, took a keen professional interest in comparative religion. In *Alice in Wonderland,* we have 'Rule 42: All persons more than a mile high to leave the Court.' Another Rule 42 crops up in the preface to *The Hunting of the Snark,* and in the same work we may read, of The Baker:

'He had forty-two boxes, all carefully packed,
With his name clearly painted on each;
But, since he omitted to mention the fact,
They were all left behind on the beach.'

Furthermore, the story-teller in *Phantasmagoria* gives his age as forty-two, although Carroll was only in his thirties when he wrote it. Finally, the price on the Hatter's hat in Tenniel's illustration of the mad tea-party is ten shillings and sixpence, which is 126 pence, and 126 is three times forty-two. There are, incidentally, forty-two illustrations by Tenniel altogether in Carroll's works.

Forty-two is also the number of:

Articles of Religion of the Church of England drawn up in 1553, which later formed the basis for the Thirty-Nine Articles

aspects of personality revealed by head bumps according to the pseudo-science of phrenology

books on stamps or stamp-collecting published in the UK in 1996

degrees of angle between rainbow and observer's shadow

demons present at the judgment of a dead person's soul in ancient Egypt

different impressions left by tyres with which Sherlock Holmes claimed to be familiar in *Priory School* by Arthur Conan Doyle

eyes in a pack of cards

gestation period in days of a ferret

governments that established the League of Nations in 1918

inches in the maximum permitted length of a baseball bat

kilometres from Dover to Calais

kilometres length of the Berlin wall

known species of the Bird of Paradise (of which you may find thirty-three in Papua New Guinea)

lines in a 'length' – theatrical slang for a portion of an actor's part equal to forty-two lines

lines of type in each column of most pages of the Gutenberg Bible,
   which is therefore sometimes called the 'forty-two-line Bible'
miles per hour for the maximum speed of a grey fox
minutes an object would take to fall when dropped into a straight
   frictionless tunnel bored through the earth. Curiously, it does not
   matter if the hole goes right through the centre of the earth and out
   the other side, or is bored at an incline to emerge wherever you
   choose, the effect of gravity guarantees that it will always take the
   same forty-two minutes to come out the other end
provinces of Ancient Egypt, called 'nomes'
staff manning the year-round stations in Antarctica
stations that the children of Israel had to pass through between Egypt
   and Sinai
teeth of a dog or wolf
teeth of a whale, according to Herman Melville in *Moby Dick*
wells that can be drilled from a single platform of an oil rig
years the Holy Grail is said to have fed Joseph of Arimathea when he was
   imprisoned by the Romans

Forty-two is also celebrated in film:
42nd Street (1933); Busby Berkeley classic musical
The 42nd Street Cavalry (1974): Dennis Weaver in a mystery romance
and book:
Forty-Two Years Amongst Indians and Eskimo by J. Hordern (1893)

■ **43**

'She may very well pass for forty-three
In the dusk with a light behind her.'
W. S. Gilbert, *Trial By Jury*, 1875

Life may begin at forty, but forty-three seems to be the age at which it
starts to deteriorate. Apart from Gilbert's snide line, we also have Robert
Browning's: *'I am forty-three years old; in prime of life, perfection of estate.'*
(Red Cotton Nightcap Country, 1873) and C. M. Yonge's, *'She looked
her full forty-three years'* (Cameos, 1979).

Forty-three is also the number of:
beans alleged to be in each cup of Nescafe
city trades depicted on the windows of Chartres Cathedral
pairs of nerves joining the central nervous system with rest of body
years the Empire State Building was the tallest in the world (1931-74, at
   the end of which it was overtaken by Sears Tower, Chicago)

■ **44**

'Again I was lucky with the Psalms; the Sunday before there had been forty-four verses; this Sunday there were forty-three, seven below the danger line.'
L. P. Hartley, *The Go-Between*, 1953

The *Oxford English Dictionary* defines a 'forty-four' as either: a) a forty-four gun ship; or b) a bicycle with a wheel forty-four inches in diameter. This seems a peculiarly unfortunate linguistic coincidence, full of opportunities for confusion and misunderstanding.

Forty-four is also the number of:
feet length of a badminton doubles court
feet length of the oars in galleys at the end of the eighteenth century
languages into which Bram Stoker's *Dracula* has been translated
times Britain has been judged to have violated the Human Rights
    Convention in the period 1960-96
years to which the oldest Tower of London raven, Jim Crow, lived

■ **45**

'Mrs Deborah no sooner observed this than she fell to squeezing and kissing, with as great raptures as sometimes inspire the sage dame of forty and five towards a youthful and vigorous bridegroom.'
Henry Fielding, *Tom Jones*

On the other hand, we have:
'A maiden of forty-five, exceedingly starched, vain and ridiculous.'
Tobias Smollett, *Humphrey Clinker*, 1771

A forty-five may be an extended-play record or the most popular handgun in the Wild West. The Colt .45 was not made until more than thirty years after the death of Samuel Colt, inventor, in 1835, of the revolving pistol. He became the most successful gunsmith in America when, in 1847, he received an order to supply 1,000 guns to the American army. Cartridge-loading revolvers first appeared in 1857, five years before Samuel Colt died. The first self-loading semi-automatic pistol arrived in 1895, and two years later, John Browning patented the automatic pistol which became the basis for the Colt .45.

Forty-five is also the number of:

bells in the carillon in the city of Mechelen, Belgium
centimetres of sleeping space allowed to convicts on board ships taking
   them from England to Australia after 1802
centimetres length of an aardvark's tongue

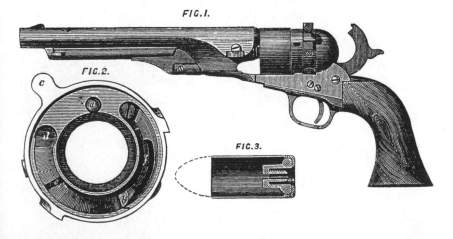

degrees in the smaller angles of a right-angled isosceles triangle
dinosaurs named by Friedrich von Huene
grams of honey made from the nectar collected by one bee in its lifetime
inches length of the nose of great bronze Buddha at Kamakura, Japan
letters in the longest word to be found in any English dictionary in 1966:
   pneumonoultramicroscopicsilicovolcanoconiosis (small particles of
   ash and dust – included in the Merriam-Webster's great Unabridged)
maximum permitted run-up for pole vault in metres
miles per hour maximum speed of an elk
species of Coccinellid beetles found in Britain
years' marriage for a sapphire anniversary

Film: *45 Fathers* (1937): comedy
Novel: *The Forty-Five* by Alexandre Dumas
Musical: *Forty-Five Minutes from Broadway* (1906) by George M. Cohan

THE COLT BREECH-LOADING
REVOLVER.

FIG.1.

FIG.2.

FIG.3.

'She's six-and-forty and I wish nothing worse to happen to any woman.'
Sir Arthur Wing Pinero, *The Second Mrs Tanqueray*, 1893

There is a beautiful little word-game to be played with the number forty-six and the King James Bible. If you count forty-six words from the beginning of Psalm 46, you will find the word 'shake' and forty-six words from the end of the same Psalm is the word 'spear'. That translation of the Bible was published in 1610, in which year Shakespeare celebrated his forty-sixth birthday; whether Shakespeare himself was involved in the translation, or whether a fellow wordsmith had hidden the birthday greeting within the Psalm on his behalf, is a matter for speculation. Now try counting up the words in the sentence you have just read and you will understand why there is a semi-colon rather than a full stop in the middle of it.

Forty-six is also the number of:
chromosomes of a human being
countries belonging to the International Bureau of Weights and
  Measures
days before anyone noticed Matisse's 'Le Bateau' was upside down at the
  Museum of Modern Art in New York
grams maximum weight of a golf ball
inches height of Michael Dunn (1935-73), co-star of 1965 film *Ship of
  Fools*
legs of *Scolopendra gigantea*, the world's biggest centipede. Although our
  calling it 'centipede' (a hundred legs) is therefore a gross overestimate,
  we do not do nearly as badly on this matter as the Germans, who call
  a centipede a *Tausendfüssler* (thousand feet)

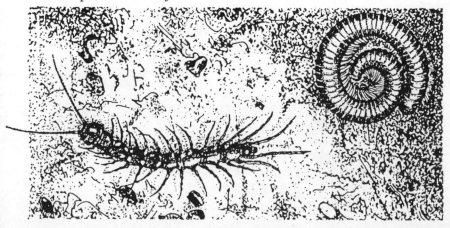

'And now let us go to the tomb of the Forty-Seven Ronins.'
Rudyard Kipling, *From Sea to Sea*, 1899

The Ronin were masterless Samurai of Naganeri Asano, who dramatically avenged their master's death on 14 December 1702. Their exploits are celebrated in several films (see below).

The AK 47 automatic rifle is perhaps the world's most famous submachine gun. The letters stand for *Avtomat Kalashnikov* – the Kalashnikov automatic, after the name of the inventor. In 1997, however, Mr Kalashnikov, now well into his eighties, said that he had always intended to gun to be used for the preservation of peace. He is not related to the *Song of the Merchant Kalashnikov* which was a mature work of Mikhail Lermontov, the Russian novelist who was shot and killed (though not by an AK 47) in a duel at the age of twenty-six in 1841.

Forty-seven is also the number of:
members of parliament arrested on 6 December 1648 for opposing the trial of Charles I
men hanged for rape in England and Wales between 1805 and 1818
metres height of the pedestal of the Statue of Liberty
Mormon temples built or under construction in the world
paragraphs on *kiddushin* (betrothal) in the *Mishnah*, the ancient Jewish law
passengers killed in crashes on British airlines 1980-89
piglets used in filming *Babe*
sounds in the Japanese language
strings on a harp
years a brown bear has lived in captivity

Films:
47 Ronin (1994): revenge in early eighteenth century Japan (*Shiijushichin no Shikaku* in the original)
The 47 Ronin, Part 1 (1942): earlier version of the above
The 47 Ronin, Part 2 (1942): more of the same

Essay: *On Completing Forty-Seven* by Thomas Hood. Sadly Hood never did: he died in 1845 at the age of forty-six

'Mr Woodhouse considered eight persons at dinner together as the utmost that his nerves could bear – and here would be a ninth – and Emma apprehended that it would be a ninth very much out of humour, at not being able to come even to Hartfield for forty-eight hours, without falling in with a dinner-party.'
Jane Austen, *Emma*, 1816. (This quotation, incidentally, is the first recorded use of the compound noun 'dinner-party'.)

The 'Forty-Eight', Johann Sebastian Bach's 48 Preludes and Fugues, properly known as *Das wohltemperierte Klavier*, is one of the most influential compositions in the history of music. They were written to demonstrate the effectiveness of 'temperament' – a method of tuning the piano keyboard to enable music to be played in any key. Essentially the system involves a compromise on many of the notes, rendering them slightly out of tune so that they will not be too far out whatever key one is playing in. (It's all to do with B flat not really being the same note as A sharp.) It is this out-of-tuneness that makes music in one key sound different from another when played on a keyboard. Bach's forty-eight are, in fact, two sets of twenty-four preludes and fugues, one in each of the twelve keys, major and minor.

The versatile divisibility of forty-eight, which is equal to 2×24, or 3×16, or 4×12, or 6×8, must be held responsible for the linguistic overkill exhibited by the words hexakisoctahedron, octakishexahedron, tetrakisdodecahedron and tetrakonta-octahedron, all of which mean the same solid body bounded by forty-eight triangular planes, as is found in the crystalline formation of diamonds. Fortunately the problem may be avoided by calling it an adamantoid.

Forty-eight is also the number of:
accidents in UK homes in 1994 involving beanbags
cards needed to play pinochle
chromosomes of great apes
constellations listed by Ptolemy
days in space for south American guppies on board Salyut 5 in 1976.
     These were the first fish in space
deaths from Creutzfeldt-Jacob Disease in the UK in 1996
letters in Bernard Shaw's logical spelling alphabet
pairs of socks received as presents by George Bush when he was vice-
     president
political divisions, known as naucraries, of the ancient Athenians

pounds weight of an elephant's heart

Every film with 'forty-eight' in the title has that number followed by the word 'hours':

The Forty-Eight Hour Mile (1970): Carrie Snodgrass in a love-triangle mystery

48 Hours (1944): World War II drama from a story by Graham Greene

48 Hours (1982): Nick Nolte and Eddie Murphy in comedy suspense

48 Hours to Acapulco (1968): gangsters and espionage

48 Hours to Live (1960): nuclear scientists are kidnapped

Book: F*orty-Eight Days Adrift* by J. Barbour (1932)

■ **49**

'In a cavern, in a canyon
Excavating for a mine,
Dwelt a miner, forty-niner
And his daughter, Clementine.'
Percy Montrose, *Clementine*, 1884

The Forty-Niners were speculators who rushed to California after gold was discovered there in 1848. By the end of 1849, California's population had increased from about 15,000 to over 100,000. San Francisco grew from a small town into a city of 25,000 people, and the busiest port on the Pacific coast, as it became the main place of arrival for hopeful prospectors from all over the world.

Forty-nine is also the number of:

balls in the British lottery

instant lottery tickets sold every second in Britain

phonetic symbols of the zhuyin zimu pronunciation alphabet, officially
promulgated in 1918 by the Chinese government

professional fights fought and won by Rocky Marciano

years of age at which your mind is in its prime: 'The body is in its prime
from thirty to five-and-thirty; the mind about forty-nine.' Aristotle,
Rhetoric, Fourth century BC

Films include:

The 49th Parallel (1941): Nazis flee through Canada trying to escape to
the USA: Raymond Massey and Michael Redgrave

The 49th Man (1953): atom bombs and espionage

Forty-Nine Days (1964): US Navy saves shipwrecked Soviet sailors

Books:

Diary of a Forty-Niner by A. T. Jackson (1906)

Experiences of a Forty-Niner by C. D. Ferguson (1888)

Log of a Forty-Niner by R. L. Hale (1900)

■ 50

'A man shouldn't fool with booze until he's fifty;
then he's a damn fool if he doesn't.'
William Faulkner, quoted in James M. Webb and
A. Wigfall Green: *William Faulkner of Oxford*, 1965

L is the Roman number for fifty and, as with all the other Roman
numerals, the letter does not stand for any particular word. Even in the
case of C (which could so easily stand for *centum*, a hundred), the
number-letter was originally only a symbol, which eventually became
identified with the letter it resembled.

Fifty is the smallest number that can be expressed in two different
ways as the sum of two squares: $50 = 1^2+7^2 = 5^2+5^2$.

Fifty is also the number of:

days in the gestation period of a mink

days the 'khamsin' wind is expected to blow through Egypt around the
month of April. A hot windstorm, its name comes from the Arabic for
fifty

height in inches of Queen Matilda, wife of William I.

inches in the maximum permitted height for a member of 'The Little

People of America' society
millimetres width of the average European condom when flat
oysters Casanova recommended eating for breakfast
pounds sterling in a 'monkey'
United States of America, since Hawaii joined the other 49 in 1959.
   Hawaii was formerly known as the Sandwich Islands, thus named by
   James Cook in honour of the fourth Earl of Sandwich, First Lord of
   the Admiralty and the first person to enjoy food between two slices of
   bread
Ways to Leave Your Lover, according to the hit song by Paul Simon, of
   which perhaps the most memorable is 'get on the bus, Gus'
years' marriage for a golden anniversary

'Fifty-fifty' indicates a perfect balance between alternatives. The fifties in
the expression clearly relate to percentages, and since percentages are
ratios rather than pure numbers we have generally excluded them from
this book. For anyone in search of a percentage, however, here is a
complete table, from 0 to 99. The figures quoted are in each case based
on recent surveys. The sample may be assumed to be from the UK unless
otherwise stated.

0% of Americans keep gloves in their glove compartments
1% of men admit to changing their underpants less than once a week
2% of adults never travel by car
3% of sexual acts referred to in soap operas are between married
   partners
4% of women registered with computer dating agencies are civil
   servants
5% of households have three or more children
6% of married women say their husbands have definitely been
   unfaithful more than once
7% of Americans eat at MacDonalds every day
8% of husbands clean the lavatories in their homes
9% of women usually take a condom with them to parties
10% of US adults are against sex education in schools
11% of US adults would like to be president
12% of the world's fishing catch is taken by the Japanese
13% of American women think themselves pretty
14% of the world's bananas come from India
15% of household expenditure goes on motoring and fares
16% of British truck-drivers think of 'nothing in particular' while
   driving
17% of the world's goat meat comes from China

18% of the world's pineapples come from Thailand
19% of Americans think O. J. Simpson is likely to go to heaven
20% of the world's carrots grow in China
21% of the world's cheese is made in America
22% of the world's beef and veal comes from the US
23% of Americans keep sunglasses in their glove compartments
24% of the world's coffee comes from Brazil
25% of a bear's weight is lost in hibernation
26% of all pasta is spaghetti
27% of all couples (married or cohabiting) have no children
28% of American men think themselves handsome
29% of the world's natural rubber comes from Malaysia
30% of cat's visits to the vet are for vaccinations
31% of the world's cucumbers and gherkins come from China
32% of the world's coconuts come from Indonesia
33% of the world's hops grow in Germany
34% of accidents requiring hospital treatment happen in the home
35% of the world's camels are in Somalia
36% of Britons call the lavatory the 'loo'
37% of the world's mules are Chinese
38% of women would end the relationship if they discovered their
    partner was unfaithful
39% of the world's salt comes from Australia
40% of US scientists believe in God and an afterlife
41% of adults say they have made love in the kitchen
42% of the world's grapefruit grows in the US
43% of women re-read their Mother's Day cards
44% of adults say they can communicate in at least one foreign language
    (but see 86%)
45% of women are happy with their breasts
46% of manual workers say they go for regular dental check-ups
47% of cats are overweight
48% of lottery participants stick to the same numbers every time
49% of marriages take place in church
50% of women describe the experience of losing their virginity as 'awful'
    or 'disappointing'
51% of US women think that men are basically gentle, kind and
    thoughtful
52% of males aged between fourteen to twenty-five never wash their own
    clothes
53% of the world's buffaloes are in India
54% of American men are concerned about foot odour
55% of women aged twenty-five to twenty-nine are married

56% of adults claim to have had sex in a field
57% of US cat owners confide in their cats over important matters
58% of nine-to-eleven-year-old American girls regularly use deodorant
59% of married women consider their husbands unromantic
60% of the population suffer from dandruff at some time in their lives
61% of men over sixteen are married
62% of adults say they have been cuddled while washing the dishes
63% of the world's mangoes grow in India
64% of men wash their hands after preparing food
65% of people hate junk mail
66% of confectionery is bought by women
67% of Americans are certain that heaven exists
68% of the world's yams come from Nigeria

69% of women over sixteen wear glasses or contact lenses
70% of British teenageres have signed at least one petition
71% of British children aged seven to fifteen can make baked beans on
   toast
72% of male teenagers tidy their rooms once a month or less
73% of dog owners have taken time off work because their pet was ill
74% of American teenagers believe in angels
75% of adults have a current account at a bank
76% of sexual offence cases are cleared up by the police
77% of women aged thirty-five to thirty-nine are married
78% of airline seats are occupied
79% of households have a video recorder
80% of females aged fourteen to twenty-five sometimes do the household
   shopping
81% of women would never consider cosmetic breast surgery

82% of men in their fifties are married
83% of the population watches at least three consecutive minutes of
    television every day
84% of dog owners would rather have their toes licked by their dog than
    by their partner
85% of convicted females are under thirty-five
86% of the population are not fluent in any foreign language
87% of Americans think they are likely to go to heaven
88% of thefts from cars are not cleared up by the police
89% of women would never have an affair with their sister's boyfriend
90% of households have a washing machine
91% of Suriname is covered by forest (the most foresty country on earth)
92% of teenage girls in Middlesex tidy their rooms at least once a week
93% of households have a telephone
94% of women aged sixteen to forty-four have no difficulty hearing
95% of adults take a magazine to bed with them
96% of women have entertained or visited friends in the last month
97% of currency notes in the US bear traces of cocaine
98% of car journeys involve some sort of careless driving
99% of fridges in America are white or almond

■ 51

*'To denote as Proof Spirit that which, at the Temperature of Fifty-one
Degrees by Fahrenheit's Thermometer, weighs exactly Twelve
Thirteenth Parts of an equal Measure of Distilled Water.'*
Act of George III, 1818

The fifty-first Psalm, known as the 'neck Psalm', which begins, in the
Latin, 'Miserere mei Deus' (Have mercy upon me, O God), was the one
traditionally set for an accused criminal to read if he was to save his neck
by claiming 'benefit of clergy', an exemption from civil law granted to
officials of the church.

Fifty-one is also the number of:
days in the gestation period of a fox
founder states of the United Nations in 1945
Grand Prix wins of Alain Prost
nursery rhymes in *Mother Goose's Melody* (1781), including 'Ding Dong,
    Bell' and 'Little Tommy Tucker'
razor sets sold by Gillette in the first year of business
years age of the oldest known orang utan, Julia, who died in November
    1992 in Rotterdam Blijdorp zoo

'She has as many diseases as two and fifty horses.'
William Shakespeare, *Taming of the Shrew*, 1623

'Quoth she "Here's but two and fifty hairs on your chin,
and one of them is white".'
William Shakespeare, *Troilus and Cressida*

Fifty-two, apart from being a favourite number of Shakespeare's, was also important in the calendar of the Mayan civilisation. They had a curious system of counting the passage of time, with one cycle of thirteen days operating concurrently with another cycle of twenty days. So if both cycles start together, it takes 260 days to get back to the beginning. And since the first multiple of 260 that is also a multiple of 365 is 18,980 (= 73×260 = 52×365), it takes fifty-two 365-day years for the Mayan calendar to get back to where it started in normal earth-years. The Mayans knew this, of course, and celebrated the beginning of a new life-cycle every fifty-two years.

Fifty-two is also the number of:
British lords reputedly kept happy by Lindi St Clair (also known as 'Miss Whiplash') in twenty years of business
cards in a pack

Eskimo dogs that pulled Roald Amundsen's supplies on his trek to the South Pole in 1911. Only eleven of the dogs returned. The explorers had shot and eaten the weakest ones when they were no longer needed
'fundamental playing errors' Charles Darrow was told Monopoly had when he submitted it to Parker Brothers in 1934
inches above the floor of the top rope around a boxing ring
varieties of condom available in Norway in 1991
weeks in a year

Films include:
52nd Street (1937): musical, not nearly as good or successful as the one ten blocks down (→42)
52 Pick-Up (1986): Ann-Margret in a tale of violence based on a book by Elmore Leonard

89 kilometres of Californian beach

*'And the sun went down, and the stars came out far over the
summer sea,
But never a moment ceased the fight of the one and the fifty-three.'*
Alfred Tennyson, *The Revenge*, 1880

The poem is a romantic account of the final battle of Sir Richard
Grenville (1541?-91) whose ship the *Revenge* was isolated off Flores and
engaged in a fifteen-hour battle with a large number of Spanish vessels
before being finally overcome. The number 'fifty-three' is an honest
enough count of the Spanish force, though Tennyson does not mention
that all but twenty of them were supply vessels, and only fifteen of the
warships joined in against the *Revenge*. Nor does he mention that the
whole battle only came about because of Grenville's stubbornness and
bad temper in insisting on not letting the Spanish get in his way, rather
than steering away from them.

In the 1890s the game of poker was popularly played with fifty-three
cards (they called it Fifty-three Deck Poker), the fifty-third card being
the joker or a blank card usually included as a spare by the makers of
packs in America. It has been suggested that the original of the game lay
in the meanness of people who did not want to see the blank card
wasted. The name given to the blank card was 'mistigris', from an old
French card-playing term which usually signified the jack of spades.

Fifty-three is also the number of:
countries in the Commonwealth
countries in which the Spice Girl had had a number one hit within six
    months of their debut
Dickin medals awarded to animals in World War Two
honorary degrees awarded to Bob Hope
the most miles ridden backwards on a unicycle
the number painted on Herbie the VW in the film *The Love Bug*
square kilometres in Bermuda
suites in Claridges Hotel (→191)

Art: 'Fifty-three Stations of the Tokaido Highway' – a set of prints by
    Hiroshige

■ 54

'Fifty-four forty or fight' was a slogan in the 1830s, later taken up by the Democrats in the 1844 presidential election campaign, during a boundary dispute between the United States and England. According to a treaty of 1818, both countries could occupy the Oregon County, lying between latitudes 42° and 52°40′ north, but in the 1830s and 40s expansionists wanted to take the whole area by force if necessary. The issue was eventually settled with a compromise placing the border between the US and Canada along the 49th parallel.

Fifty-four is also the number of:
articles of clothing bought by the average American female each year
basketball riots in the US 1960-72
cards in a pack (including jokers)
inches width of a standard double bed
percentage of world's buffaloes in India
sections of the Pentateuch known as Sedra (or Sedrah) one of which is
    read in the Synagogue on the Sabbath morning service

■ 55

The fifty-five gallon oil-drum has had a profound influence on the development of civilisation. Quite apart from its primary duty in fuelling the allied forces in the second world war, the container itself was then used for a variety of purposes. It was the basic building block for a large number of bridges; it enabled the construction of solar-powered showers at many military bases; and, last but by no means least, it was the inspiration behind the development of the West Indian steel band.

Fifty-five is also the number of:
cases of wife-sale recorded in Britain 1840-80
days it took Johann Hurlinger to walk from Vienna to Paris on his hands
    in the nineteenth century
inches in the height of Charles I
murders in Belgrade in 1996 (→40)
ounces weight of the average human liver

---

pounds of pasta eaten each year by the average Italian
years' marriage for an emerald anniversary

Film:
Fifty-Five Days at Peking (1963): Charlton Heston and David Niven in
the Boxer rebellion

Books:
Flying Fifty-Five by Edgar Wallace (1922)
Fifty-Five Years at Oxford, by G. B. Grundy (1945)

■ 56

'The cat goes with young fifty-six days.'
Oliver Goldsmith, *Animated Nature*, 1774

Fifty-six is a number that could be of interest to anyone investigating the
derivation of the phrase 'cold enough to freeze the balls off a brass
monkey'. Although nobody can be certain, one theory is that the balls in
question are cannonballs and 'monkey' was a slang term for the stand on
which the cannonballs were piled. In conditions of extreme cold, any
stand made of brass would contract more than the iron of the
cannonballs, thus causing the balls to fall off. In other words, freezing the
balls off the brass monkey. Unfortunately, there is a dearth of examples
of brass cannonball stands to support this theory. And where does the
fifty-six come in? Well, if you make a perfect pyramid of cannonballs,
there will be one at the top, supported by three on the level below, and
six on the level below that, then ten, fifteen, twenty-one and so on. So a
six-storey cannonball pile will have a total of 1+3+6+10+15+21 = 56
cannonballs.

Fifty-six is also the number of:
days it takes a plucked hair to reappear
journalists killed in action around the world in 1993
kilometres the average pencil can write
minutes in the maximum length of a polo game
storeys in Canary Wharf, Europe's tallest occupied building
times Salman Rusdie is said to have changed his address in the six
    months after the fatwa
years reign of Henry III

57

*'The lunches of fifty-seven years had caused his chest
to slip down into the mezzanine floor.'*
P. G. Wodehouse, *The Heart of a Goof,* 1926

Fifty-seven is a number that crops up more often than it ought in great disasters. There were fifty-seven people killed by Woo Bum Kong on 28 April 1982 in Sang-Namdo, South Korea, in the world's worst massacre by a single killer; there were fifty-seven people killed in the eruption of Mount St Helens volcano in the United States in 1980 after it had been inactive for the previous 123 years. Fifty-seven was also the number of buckets taken on the Victorian Exploring Expedition from Melbourne, Australia, in 1860 by the team led by Robert O'Hara Burke. They also took twenty-five camels, eighty pairs of shoes, twenty camp beds and thirty cabbage tree hats. The expedition was a disaster.

More auspicious fifty-sevens include the number of:
books on dentistry published in the UK in 1996
grams of flour eaten by the average Briton each week
grams of salt eaten each day by the average horse
Heinz varieties, allegedly – though there were already over sixty when the
    'Heinz 57' catch-phrase was adopted
police officers in the siege at Glenrowan, Australia, in 1880, that led to
    the capture of Ned Kelly
women serving jail sentences in England and Wales for burglary at the
    beginning of 1997
world billiard records held by Walter Lindrum when he retired
    undefeated in 1950

58

*'He pretended that he had cleaned up all the
tough guys on Fifty-eighth Street.'*
J. T. Farrell, *Young Lonigan,* 1936

Fifty-eight is a number associated with extremes of temperature. For −58°C is the average temp of Polus Nedostupnosti in Antarctica – the coldest place on earth – and +58°C is the highest temperature ever recorded, at Al Aziziyah, Libya in 1922.

Fifty-eight is also the number of:
cities in Britain

different languages taught in India's schools
facets in a 'brilliant cut' diamond
megatons of a hydrogen bomb exploded by the USSR in 1961, the
    largest ever built
novels written by Rider Haggard
ships sunk by the 1867 hurricane in the West Indies

■ 59

'Good engine this. We're dong fifty-nine or an unripe sixty.'
Compton Mackenzie, *The Early Life of Sylvia Scarlett*, 1919

Fifty-nine is a number with good royal connections, for it is the number of kings and queens of Sweden, and also the number of years George III of England reigned.

Fifty-nine is also the number of:
countries in the world that drive on the left
days in the rotation period of the planet Mercury
minutes from the opening bell to the finish of a fifteen-round boxing
    match
percentage of nitrogen in a fart
square miles of the British Virgin islands
tons of Berlin wall shipped to US in the year following its demolition

Book: *Fifty-Nine Icosahedra* (1938) by H. S. M. Coxeter *et al.*

■ 60

'Here I sit, alone and sixty,
Bald and fat and full of sin,
Cold I sit and loud the cistern,
As I read the Harpic tin.'
Alan Bennett, *Place Names of China*

The ancient Sumerians and ancient Chinese both did much of their counting in a system to base sixty. The Chinese calendar, in particular, operates according to cycles of sixty years, beginning in 2637 BC, when the legendary Emperor Huangdi invented it. So the seventy-eighth cycle began in 1983 (2637+1983 = 4620, which is 60×77). The sixty seconds in a minute, sixty minutes in an hour and 360 degrees in a circle are all relics of ancient base-sixty counting systems. Plutarch was impressed by the number sixty and believed that crocodiles laid sixty eggs, which

incubated for sixty days, before hatching into baby crocs that lived for sixty years.

Sixty is also the number of:
degrees in each angle of an equilateral triangle
floral arrangements sent to Gracelands each anniversary of Presley's death
wives of Khaled Ashta of Egypt. He divorced the sixtieth in 1995 and
    was reported to be looking for a sixty-first. The marriages lasted
    between forty-eight hours and three years
years' marriage for a diamond anniversary

■ 61

*'She has thrown her husband out of the house sixty-one times, but he
always returned. It looks as if she put too much top-spin on him.'*
Punch, 1934

61 Cygni is the 'flying star', the first star other than the sun whose
distance from the earth was measured with any accuracy (by Friedrich
Bessel in 1838). It is also interesting to note that one person in every
sixty-one in Britain is called 'Smith'.

Sixty-one is also the number of:
centimetres above the ground Louis Breguet's helicopter rose on the first
    manned helicopter flight in 1907
centimetres per hour for the speed of a snail
points needed to win a game of 8-ball pool
square miles in Liechtenstein

■ 62

Sixty-two is an important number in the history of paying workers piece-rates. An example of this dating back to the middle ages was the practice of paying scribes by the 'pecia' (piece), each being precisely sixteen columns, each of sixty-two lines with thirty-two characters to the line.

Sixty-two is also the number of:
hours a week the average British mother spends on household tasks
hours a week the average British person over fifteen spends asleep
references to 'camel' in the Bible
self-portraits by Rembrandt
tombs that have been discovered in the Valley of the Kings at Luxor
years of age of the oldest recorded horse

Sixty-two is also the opus number the French composer Eric Satie gave to his first composition.

■ 63

'A lady in the virgin bloom of sixty-three.'
Oliver Goldsmith, *The Citizen of the World*, 1762

Sixty-three, being one less than the sixth power of two, is the number of distinct non-empty sets that can be formed from a collection of six objects. Or, to put it in a less mathematical formulation, it is the number of distinct omelettes you can choose to make from one carton of six eggs. (If you work it out, they are six one-egg omelettes, fifteen with two eggs, twenty with three eggs, fifteen with four eggs, six with five eggs, and one with all six.)

Sixty-three is also the number of:
aeroplanes of the Royal Flying Corps at the start of World War I
articles of Magna Carta
gates to the palace in Bangkok of King Rama I of Thailand (reigned
    1782-1809)
heliports in the United States
inches of Britain's longest moustache
people fatally shot in the UK in 1994

possible arrangements of the dots in the Braille system
sections (tractates) of the Talmud
types of wren, mostly living in Asia and America; only one type lives in
    Europe
years of Victoria's reign
years of age of Rosanna Dalla Corta when she gave birth in 1994 – at the
    time the oldest woman to have a child. Her record lasted only three
    years, when it was broken by a 66-year-old who had lied about her age
    when applying for fertility treatment

■ 64

'Will you still need me, will you still feed me,
When I'm sixty-four?'
John Lennon and Paul McCartney, 1967

Sixty-four, as the sixth power of two, is simultaneously a square (of eight)
and a cube (of four). Its capacity to be halved so many times makes it a
natural number to crop up whenever symmetry or divisibility is required.
The sixty-four squares of a chessboard and the sixty-four hexagrams of
the *I Ching* are both examples of the inherently playful nature of the
number, though it was the Indians who took its playfulness most
seriously with the sixty-four arts of loving taught in the *Kama Sutra*.

Sixty-four is also the number of:
Germans expelled from Great Britain between 1907 and 1914 for
    procuring and prostitution
grams of tinned soup consumed by the average Briton each week
inches height of James Madison, the shortest US President
kilometres per hour top speed of a kangaroo or an ostrich

lifts on the London underground system
squares on a chessboard
titles in grand slam tennis tournaments won by Margaret Court (twenty-
    four singles, twenty-one women's doubles, nineteen mixed doubles)

'As a rule, the male is generative up to the age of sixty-five, and to the age of forty-five the female is capable of conception.'
Aristotle, *History of Animals*, fourth century BC

Sixty-five is a number with good connections to clothing. It is the number of costumes worn by Elizabeth Taylor in the filming of *Cleopatra*, and also the maximum number of minks needed to make one average-sized coat.

Sixty-five is also the number of:
hairs shed daily by the average person
inches in the height of the average British fully grown male in 1900
slaves owned by Patrick Henry in 1775 when he said: 'Give me liberty or
    give me death.'

■ **66**

'Sixty-six years ago a vast number both of travellers and stay-at-homes were in this condition.'
Charles Dickens, *Barnaby Rudge*, 1841

Sixty-six is an old German card game, mentioned in the 1857 edition of *Hoyle's Games* as 'Sechs und Sechzig'. By the end of the nineteenth century it had established itself in England. In Islamic counties, however, the number is more highly respected as it is the numerological value (in one ancient system at least) of the name of Allah.

Sixty-six is also the number of:
Books in the King James Bible
clickety-click in Bingo
combat missions flown in Korea in 1952 by Edwin 'Buzz' Aldrin
football riots in the US 1960-72
grammes of oranges eaten by the average Briton each week
'Nylon 66' the name given to the original type of nylon, so-called
    because both chemicals used in making it had six carbon atoms
symphonies of the Austrian composer Franz Anton Hoffmeister
    (1742-1815)

Song: 'Get Your Kicks on Route 66' by Bob Troup, 1946

---

98 countries watched 'Dallas' on TV

■ 67

'You've sixty-seven and you don't cake.'
Rudyard Kipling, *They*, 1904. (The sixty-seven in the quotation were sixty-seven bullocks, and 'cake' means 'to feed on cake'.)

Sixty-seven is the number of African elephants needed to equal the weight of a Boeing 747 Jumbo jet.

Sixty-seven is also the number of:
knock-out wins by Jimmy Wilde, the 'Mighty Atom', a record for British boxing
lines in Shakespeare's poem 'The Phoenix and the Turtle'
novels by Agatha Christie (plus sixteen books of short stories and sixteen plays (→83)
operatic roles sung by Enrico Caruso
ships of the Spanish Armada that returned to Spain of the 130 that set out
US Air Force personnel court-martialled for adultery in 1996 (sixty male and seven female)

■ 68

'It was nothing but a watering depot in the midst of a
stretch of sixty-eight miles.'
Mark Twain, *Roughing It*, 1872

Sixty-eight has sporting connections, for it is the maximum length in centimetres of a badminton racquet and also the maximum width in metres of a rugby pitch.

Sixty-eight is also the number of:
boat race wins for Oxford (1829-1996)
Germans expelled from Great Britain between 1906 and 1914 for 'housebreaking and frequenting'
years of hiccups in the longest recorded attack

Film: *'68* (1987): a Hungarian opens a café in San Francisco

'There are nine and sixty ways of constructing tribal lays,
And-every-single-one-of-them-is-right!'
Rudyard Kipling, *Ballads and Barrack-Room Ballads,* 1893

Sixty-nine, or *Soixante-neuf,* is defined in the *OED* as 'simultaneous cunnilingus and fellatio', or by P. Perret in *Tableaux Vivants* (1888) as 'this divine variant of pleasure'. According to the citations in the *OED,* we continued referring to it in French until 1973, though five years later we were already joking about it: 'When I first met him, I thought 69 was a bottle of Scotch' (from the *Guardian Weekly,* 1978). The number sixty-nine is also the only number whose square (4,761) and cube (328,509) between them use each of the digits from 0 to 9 once and once only.

Sixty-nine is also the number of:
airports in Azerbaijan
decibels of a loud snore
kilometres per hour top speed at which a shark has been timed
people killed at Sharpeville, South Africa, in 1960 when police opened
    fire on anti-apartheid protesters
square miles of Washington DC

Films include:
Locker Sixty-Nine (1963): Paul Daneman in detective story
69 Minutes (1977): feature film

■ 70

'The true artist will let his wife starve, his children go barefoot, his
mother drudge for his living at seventy, sooner than work at anything
but his art.'
George Bernard Shaw, *Man and Superman,* 1903

Seventy is the biblical 'threescore and ten' years of our allotted lifespan, but that is far from being its only significant appearance in the Old Testament. Indeed the Greek translation of the Old Testament was supposedly carried out by seventy scholars (seventy-two according to some sources), which is why it is referred to as the *Septuagint.* Seventy was also the number of men who accompanied Moses to Mount Sinai, the number of years the Babylonians were in exile and the number of days Moses was mourned.

Seventy is also the number of:

days it took in total to mummify an ancient Egyptian. The word 'mummy', incidentally, comes from *Mumiya,* an Arabic word for an embalmed body

inches height of the average fully grown British male in 1996

O-level examinations passed by Francis Thomason of West London. Explaining his success at passing more O-levels than anyone else, Dr Thomason stressed the importance of wearing comfortable slippers for an exam

Russians and Poles expelled from Great Britain 1906-14 for crimes against the person

William Byrd's compositions for harpsichord included in the 'Fitzwilliam Virginal Book' (*c.* 1625)

years' marriage for a platinum anniversary

■ 71

If you ever need to know the cube of seventy-one, it's very easy to remember. Just write down the odd numbers from 3 to 11 one after another: 357,911, and that's it.

Seventy-one is also the number of:

grams of pork eaten each year by the average Briton

men burnt at the stake in Seville for sodomy and bestiality between 1567 and 1616

the most full hours spent standing on one leg

times a year the average Londoner makes love

Film: *71 Fragments of a Chronology of Chance* (1994): avant-garde Austrian murder mystery

Autobiography: *Seventy-one Not Out* by W. Caffyn (1899)

■ 72

'Furthermore, some men and some women produce female offspring and some male, as for instance in the story of Hercules, who among all his two and seventy children is said to have begotten but one girl.'
Aristotle, *History of Animals,* fourth century BC

Seventy-two was a mystical number in the Middle Ages, when it was claimed in some circles that the name of God had seventy-two letters (though others maintained that He had seventy-two names). Part of the evidence for this belief was three consecutive verses of the Book of Exodus, each of which (in the original Hebrew) comprised exactly seventy-two letters. On the other hand, one might suppose the mystical significance of seventy-two was arrived at more simply by multiplying the three of the Trinity by the twenty-four hours in a day.

Seventy-two is also the number of:
data collectors employed at the Winbledon Lawn Tennis Championships
    in 1997
earthquakes around the world in 1996
executions personally ordered by Robespierre
heartbeats per minute for an average adult
holes in most professional golf tournaments
letters in the Cambodian alphabet
points to an inch in type-setters' measurements
years reign of Louis XIV of France

■ **73**

'Seventy-three' or 'seventy-threes' is American slang for 'best regards' or 'goodbye'. This apparently comes from the habit of Morse code operators to use almost random abbreviations for commonly used expressions. So 'seventy-three' was goodbye and 'twenty-two' was kisses.

Seventy-three is also the number of:
allied supply ships under the protection of the Dover Patrol sunk in
    World War II out of 125,000 total
British killed at Battle of Lexington and Concord, 19 April 1775, the
    opening battle of the American Revolution
islands in Ryukyu group of Japan
liberal democracies among the world's 192 sovereign states in 1995

Film: *Winchester '73* (1950), with James Stewart

■ **74**

'Seventy-four guineas, Henry. Seventy-four bloody lovely guineas.
Just wait till we tell Mr van Huyten about this.'
Stan Barstow, *A Kind of Loving,* 1960

Seventy-four is the number of:
boat race wins for Cambridge (1929-1997)
inches length of a standard double bed

minutes of sound a CD is required to be able to hold
times Clive Lloyd captained the West Indies at cricket

■ 75

'Listen, my children, and you shall hear
Of the midnight ride of Paul Revere
On the eighteenth of April in Seventy-five.'
Henry Wadsworth Longfellow, *Paul Revere's Ride*

Seventy-five has two connections with altitude: it is the number of
kilometres above the earth's surface where space officially starts and it is
also the number of armed helicopters in the Indian air force.

Seventy-five is also the number of:
paces taken a minute when marching slow time
provinces of Turkey
towns in the worls called 'Waterloo', many of which were founded by
    men who had fought in the battle in 1815

Books:
The Cornutor of Seventy-Five (anon, *c.*1750). A cornutor is a cuckold-
    maker – one who cornutes, or dallies with other men's wives
Seventy-five years Old Virginia by J. H. Clairborne, 1904
75 Brooke Street by P. Fitzgerald, 1867

■ 76

'Lady Biddy Porpoise, a lethargick virgin of seventy-six.'
Samuel John (in *The Idler*, No. 53, 1759)

Seventy-six is the number of years between successive visits of Halley's
comet (or about seventy-six years and thirty-seven days to be less
imprecise). When it passed close to earth in 1682 it was observed by
Flamsteed, Halley and Hevelius. Halley calculated its orbit and correctly
identified it with the comet that had appeared in 1607 and 1531. He
predicted that it would return in 1757 (when he would have been 101
years old). In fact, it turned up almost two years late, a delay blamed on
disturbances caused by other planets. Its next visit in 1835 was on
schedule, and its 1910 appearance was calculated to within two days.
Early twentieth-century astronomers traced the history of its sightings
back to 240 BC, with other recorded appearances in 87 BC, 11 BC, AD 66,
AD 141 and then a long break until 989 and 1066, on which occasion it

may be seen depicted on the Bayeux Tapestry.

Seventy-six is also the number of:
deaths in the film *Rambo* (of which only one is an American)
inches height of Lincoln, the tallest US President
men found guilty of rape in England and Wales between 1805 and 1818
trombones that led the big parade

■ 77

'*At seventy-seven, it is time to be in earnest.*'
Samuel Johnson, *A Journey to the Western Isles of Scotland*, 1775

Seventy-seven is the number of:
inches of snow falling in one day in January 1997 on the village of
    Montague, NY State – US record
provinces in the Philippines
Russians and Poles expelled from Great Britain 1906-14 for
    'Housebreaking and frequenting'
times a year the average British adult makes love

Film: *77 Park Lane* (1931): Gambling and blackmail in Mayfair, based
    on the play by Walter Hackett
Book: *77 Dream Songs* (1964) by John Berryman
TV series: *77 Sunset Strip*

■ 78

Seventy-eight is a good age to attain: it was the age at which Lord
Palmerston became the oldest former British prime minister to be cited
as co-respondent in a divorce case; it is also the greatest number of years
to which an Indian elephant is known to have lived.

Seventy-eight is also the number of:
chromosomes of a chicken
days record for circumnavigating the world by bicycle
feet in the length of a tennis court
gogo bars in Bangkok in 1995
revolutions per minute of an old gramophone record (discontinued in
    1958)

'*Julia:* What is Dr Paramore's number in Savile Row?
Charteris: Seventy-nine.'
G. B. Shaw, *Philanderer* in *Plays Unpleasant*, 1898

Seventy-nine is also the number of:
different names for the dragonfly in US dialects
episodes of *Star Trek* in the first three seasons 1966-68
years life expectancy in Japan, the world's highest in any major nation
    (though some sources give the life expectancy in Liechtenstein as
    eighty-one and the CIA World Fact Book lists the figure in Andorra
    as nearly ninety-one)

Film: *79 AD* (1960): Roman gladiator story

'*A coachman may be on the very amicablest terms with
eighty mile o' females, and yet nobody think that he ever
means to marry any vun of them.*'
Charles Dickens, *Pickwick Papers*, 1837

Eighty is also the number of:
chains in a mile
days around the world in Jules Verne's novel
dollars per head in the gross national product of Mozambique, the
    world's lowest
grammes of pickles and sauces eaten by the average Briton each week
percentage of the world's silk from China
soldiers in a Roman century (the other 20 were in administrative roles)
victories of Baron von Richthofen, the record for World War I

Film: *80 Steps to Jonah* (1969): Mickey Rooney in a tale of theft and
    mistaken identity

■ 81

'*It was the afternoon of my eighty-first birthday, and I was in bed with my catamite when Ali announced that the archbishop had come to see me.*'
Anthony Burgess, *Earthly Powers*, 1980, opening sentence

Eighty-one, which is nine squared, is the number of squares on a board for playing Shogi, the Japanese form of chess. It is also the number of stable elements (those having atomic numbers 1 to 42, 44-60, 62-83), and the number of passengers on a Boeing 707 who were killed by lightning in Maryland USA on 8 December 1963.

Film: *The 81st Blow* (1975): documentary on oppression during World War II

■ 82

Eighty-two kilometres is the distance between West and East, with East further west than West. That paradoxical statement becomes clear when you measure the shortest distance from Alaska – now indisputably part of Western civilisation – to Russia. America, incidentally, bought Alaska from Russia in 1867 for $7,200,000, which is somewhat less than the film *North to Alaska* (with John Wayne and Stewart Grainger) cost to make ninety-three years later.

Eighty-two is also the number of:
metres depth at the deepest point of Lake Victoria
kilograms weight of a caber
kilometres in the length of Jamaica from north to south
lighthouses controlled by Trinity House lighthouse authority
novels by Erle Stanley Gardner in which Perry Mason solves a case
recorded accidents involving beds in the UK in 1994
species of yabby, an Australian crayfish
temples restored by the Emperor Augustus

■ 83

In 1950 there were eighty-three cities in the world with more than a million people. Rome is believed to have been the first city to reach the million mark, sometime around the second century BC. Angkor (now in Cambodia) and Hangchow (China) may have reached a million in the early Middle Ages, but there were no million-plus cities anywhere at the beginning of the nineteenth century. London and Paris then became the first modern cities to reach that mark. There are now almost 300 cities (→280) with populations over one million, nine of them in the US.

Eighty-three is also the number of:
books written by Agatha Christie (sixty-seven novels and sixteen short
    story collections)
days Harry S. Truman served as Vice President before Roosevelt died
primary schools in St Lucia
recorded different spellings of 'Shakespeare' by his contemporaries
television sets per square kilometre in the UK

Film: *83 Hours 'Til Dawn* (1990): made-for-TV kidnap drama

■ 84

'On this very second of October, he had dismissed James Forster, because that youth had brought him shaving-water at eighty-four degrees Fahrenheit instead of eighty-six.'
Jules Verne, *Around the World in Eighty Days*, 1873

Eighty-four is also the number of:
centimetres height of women's high hurdles
days Calbraith P. Rodgers took to make the first flight across the
    United States in 1911
earth years in one orbit of Uranus around the sun
livery companies in London
miles length of the world's longest traffic jam – in Japan in 1990
square kilometres in Lisbon

Films include:
84 Charing Cross Road (1986): Anthony Hopkins and Anne Bancroft in
    the story by Helene Hanff
84 Charlie Mopic (1989): Vietnam war story

■ 85

Eighty-five may be associated with immoral behaviour – for it is the number of Germans expelled from Great Britain from 1907-14 for brothel keeping; it is the number of lashes to which a Tehran bride was sentenced in September 1995 for dancing with men at her wedding; and it is the number of prostitutes, of the 3,103 examined by the Metropolitan Police in 1837-38, who could read without difficulty.

Eighty-five is also the number of films made by Bette Davis and the grammes of cakes and pastries eaten by the average Briton each week.

■ 86

is the number of metres below sea level of Death Valley California, the lowest point in the Western world.

It is also the atomic number of Radon, and the number of:
centimetres of rain and other precipitation that fall on an average spot on the earth's surface each year
deaths at the storming of the Branch Dravidians in Waco 1993
square miles of Elba
stories in the first volume of Grimm's *Fairy Tales* (and another seventy in volume two)

■ 87

is the 'Four score and seven years ago' referred to by Abraham Lincoln at the start of his Gettysburg Address.

It is also the New York police department precinct number in the Ed McBain series and the number of:
cases against Britain heard by the European Court of Human Rights 1960-69
hours of music composed by Verdi
miles diameter of the biggest meteorite craters (in Canada and South Africa)

■ 88

'Eighty-eight . . . gied you . . . E'en monie a plack, and monie a peck, Ye ken yoursels, for little feck.'
Robert Burns, *Elegy on 1788*, 1789. (Feck is what you need if you are not to be considered feckless.)

Eighty-eight must be the only number to have had a town named after it. In the US Presidential election of 1948, the voting figures for one small town in Kentucky showed eighty-eight people voting for Truman and eighty-eight for Dewey. From that moment on, the town has been known as 'Eighty-eight'.

Eighty-eight is also the number of:
consecutive baseball games won by UCLA Bruins between 1971 and
    1974
constellations in the sky
earth days in one year of the planet Mercury
feet per minute to equal one mile per hour
keys on a pianoforte

■ 89

Eighty-nine is an important number for California, for it is the number
of kilometres of beach along the state's Grand Strand, as well as being the
number of Californian condors in the world in 1994.

Eighty-nine is also the atomic number of Actinium and the number of
feet in height of the columns at the Temple of Jupiter in Baalbek.

■ 90

Ninety is a sporty number, on both sides of the Atlantic. It is the number
of minutes in a (British) football game as well as being the distance in
feet between the bases in baseball.

Ninety is also the number of:
degrees in a right angle
executions in Saudi Arabia in the first four months of 1995
pupils per teacher in primary schools in the Central African Republic
    (1992) – the world's worst ratio
women in Turkey seduced by Mozart's Don Giovanni
years of age at which Sarah conceived Isaac

Films include:
90 Degrees in the Shade (1966): love and corruption in Czechoslovakia
90 Days (1986): Canadian comedy romance

Placename:
'Ninety Mile Desert', a limestone area in South Australia and Victoria

■ 91

Ninety-one degrees Fahrenheit is the temperature at which the egg of
the mallee fowl incubates. The male digs a hole for the egg in winter

and makes a compost heap to generate heat. He regulates the temperature by adding or removing sand from the heap to keep it at a constant 91°F.

Ninety-one is also the number of:
centimetres of rain that fell at Crowhamhurst, Queensland, on 3 February 1893, the highest rainfall in a day recorded in Australia
days within which the government promises to repay the holder of a treasury bill
fatalities at the bombing of the King David Hotel in Jerusalem on 22 July 1946
kilograms weight for the lower limit of the super-heavyweight class in amateur boxing
people killed by handguns in Switzerland in 1990

■ 92

There are ninety-two naturally occurring chemical elements and about another twenty that have been created in laboratory experiments, but sometimes they have been so unstable that there is argument about whether they existed. The early history of the chemical elements was one of constant miscounts and recounts. The ancients knew twelve of the elements, but did not know they were elements. In the eighteenth century, Lavoisier listed thirty-three elements, but seven of them were not elements at all. A total of seventy-six elements were added to the original twelve between 1557 and 1925, with a further twenty-one discovered, created or argued about since 1939.

Ninety-two is also the number of:
countries with capital punishment
miles of open shelving in the Cambridge University Library
people killed by hailstones in Gopalganj, Bangladesh, 14 April 1986

Films include:
92 in the Shade (1976): fishing rivalry in Florida Keys
92 Grosvenor Square (1985): World War II spy story with David McCallum and Hal Holbrook

Book:
Ninety-two Days by Evelyn Waugh, 1934

■ 93

Ninety-three is the number of minutes it took to assemble the body of a Model T Ford on the production line. When the Model T was first produced in 1908 its price was $850. The introduction of the world's first production line cut the assembly time from 12½ worker-hours to just over 1½ and by 1913 the price had dropped to $500. It was $390 in 1915 and when, by 1925, the price had dropped to $260, motoring was at last within the reach of the average American family. Between 1908 and 1926 the Model T came in one colour: black.

Ninety-three is also the number of:
countries in which Citibank has offices
masses written by Giovanni Palestrina
Test matches in which Sir Garfield Sobers played
times Allan Border captained Australia in Test matches
times Italy has been found in breach of the European Convention on
    Human Rights from 1960-96

Novel: *Ninety-Three* by Victor Hugo (set in the year 1793)

■ 94

Few people realise that the number of provinces in Bolivia is identical to the number of State Parks in Michigan. That number is ninety-four, which is also the atomic number of plutonium and the number of:

baseball games won by Babe Ruth in his major-league career
inches diameter of the Hubble Space Telescope
the usual page on which items in the British satirical magazine *Private
    Eye* are allegedly continued
people on board James Cooke's ship the *Endeavour* in 1768

■ 95

On 31 October 1517 Martin Luther nailed his 'Ninety-five Theses' on the door of the Castle church in Wittenberg. They were statements attacking abuses of the Roman Catholic church, particularly the practice of selling indulgences, and resulted in Luther being excommunicated and declared a heretic by Pope Leo X in 1521.

Ninety-five is also the number of:
kilometres per hour in the maximum speed of a dragonfly, the world's

fastest insect
sons of peers killed in the First World War by the end of 1914
Windows 95, the computer graphical user interface (GUI) launched by
Microsoft at the end of 1995

■ 96

*'And there were ninety and six pomegranates on a side; and all the
pomegranates upon the network were an hundred round about.'*
Jeremiah 52:23

Ninety-six is also the number of:
different conversations that can be carried on two pairs of telephone
wires thanks to the process of 'carrier transmission'
eggs eaten each year by average Briton
height in miles of the angel whose teachings are recorded in the heretical
Book of Elkesai
metropolitan departments of France
minutes Sputnik 1, the first artificial satellite, took to orbit the earth
storeys of Petronas Towers, Kuala Lumpur
Test matches played by Rodney Marsh
victories of Napoleon celebrated on the inner walls of the Arc de
Triomphe

Book: *My First Ninety-six Years*, an autobiography of the British
politician Emanuel Shinwell

■ 97

'Ninety-seven sixpenn'orths of gin-and-water.'
Charles Dickens, *Sketches by Boz*, 1836-37

Ninety-seven is the number of:
baseball riots in the US from 1960-72
cigarettes smoked per week by the average British female smoker
minutes it takes the average person walking briskly to use up the number
of calories in a malted milk shake
passengers on the Hindenburg airship when it exploded on 6 May 1937,
of whom thirty-five died
pounds weight of the weakling in Charles Atlas advertisements who gets
sand kicked in his face
volcanic islands in the Bonin Islands group southeast of Japan

■ 98

Ninety-eight is a significant number in the history of ballooning. In 1937, Jean Piccard, who with his twin brother Auguste was one of the pioneers of high altitude flying in balloons, made the first manned ascent with multiple balloons. He went up in a 'gondola' (an airtight passenger compartment) lifted by ninety-eight balloons each 1.5 metres in diameter.

Ninety-eight is also the number of:
countries that showed *Dallas* on TV
people per square kilometre in Gambia, Guatemala and Malawi
teeth of the priodont armadillo, according to Owen in 1854
tiles in Scrabble

Book: *The Trail of '98: A Northland Romance* by Robert William Service

■ 99

'Genius is one per cent inspiration and 99 per cent perspiration.'
Thomas Alva Edison

Ninety-nine is what doctors ask you to say when they want you to vocalise with an open throat, and what ice-cream van salesmen ask you to say if you want a chocolate flake stuck into your cornet.

Ninety-nine is also the number of:
centimetres of rain that falls on average in a year in the Bahamas
days Frederick III reigned in Germany in 1888
days it took Sir Vivian Fuchs to become the first man to cross Antarctica
    in 1957-58
Most Beautiful Names of God, other than Allah, for Muslims
members of the New Zealand parliament
the 'Ninety-Nines', an organisation of women pilots founded by Amelia
    Earhart in 1929, which still exists
warships commanded by Germany in World War I

years of age at which the prophet Abraham was circumcised (*'And Abraham was ninety years old and nine when he was circumcised in the flesh of his foreskin,'* Genesis 17:24)

years of the lease Britain had on Hong Kong that ran out in June, 1997

Ninety-nine is also a popular number in film titles, including:

The Ninety and Nine (1922): silent melodrama

99 River Street (1953): boxer struggles to clear his name of murder

99 Women (1969): lesbianism and brutality in a women's jail

99 and 44/100 Percent Dead (1974): black comedy in gangland

■ 100

'There is not one in a hundred of either sex who is not taken in when they marry.'

Jane Austen, *Mansfield Park*, 1814

One hundred, being such a fundamental number in our counting system, is chosen, more often than not, as the number of small currency units in one large currency unit. The following table tells the tale. The first column gives the small unit of currency; the second column is what 100 of these amount to, and the third column is the country of which these are the currency units. (For those countries that have 1,000 small units in a large one, →1,000.)

There are 100:	in a:	in:
cents	dollar	USA, Caribbean, Belize, Brunei, Canada, New Zealand, Fiji, Guyana, Australia, Liberia, Solomon Islands, Zimbabwe
puls	afghani	Afghanistan
centimes	dinar	Algeria
qintars	lek	Albania
lwei	kwanza	Angola
centavos	peso	Argentina, Bolivia, Cuba, Dominican Republic, Guinea-Bissau, Mexico, Philippines
luma	dram	Armwnia
groschen	schilling	Austria
gopik	manat	Azerbaijan
chetrums	ngultrum	Bhutan
thebe	pula	Botswana
centimes	franc	France, Belgium, Benin, Burundi,

		Cameroon, Djibouti, Guinea, Madagascar, Rwanda, Switzerland
fils	dinar	Bahrain
poiska	taka	Bangladesh
centavos	cruzado	Brazil
stotinki	lev	Bulgaria
pyas	kyat	Burma
sen	riel	Cambodia
centavos	escudo	Cape Verde, Portugal
jiao	yüan	China
centimos	colon	Costa Rica
paras	kuna	Croatia
cents	pound	Cyprus
haleru	koruna	Czech Republic
øre	krone	Denmark, Norway
dirhams	riyal	Dubai, Qatar
centavos	sucre	Ecuador
piastres	pound	Egypt, Lebanon
centavos	colon	El Salvador
senti	kroon	Estonia
cents	birr	Ethiopia
penniä	markka	Finland
butut	dalasi	Gambia
pfennigs	mark	Germany
pesewas	cedi	Ghana
lepta	drachma	Greece
centavos	quetzal	Guatemala
centimes	gourde	Haiti
centavos	lempira	Honduras
filler	forint	Hungary
aurar	króna	Iceland
paisa	rupee	India, Pakistan
sen	rupiah	Indonesia
rials	toman	Iran
pence	punt	Irish Republic
agorot	shekel	Israel
cents	shilling	Kenya
att	kip	Laos
cents	lat	Latvia
lisente	loti	Lesotho
kopeks	rouble	Lithuania, Russia
avos	pataca	Macao
tambala	kwacha	Malawi

sen	ringgit	Malaysia
laari	rufiyaa	Maldives
cents	lira	Malta
khoums	ouguiya	Mauritania
cents	rupee	Mauritius
mongos	tugrik	Mongolia
francs	dirham	Morocco
centavos	metical	Mozambique
paisa	rupee	Nepal
cents	gulden	Netherlands, Surinam
centavos	córdoba	Nicaragua
cobo	naira	Nigeria

jun/chon	won	North/South Korea
centesimos	balboa	Panama
toea	kina	Papua New Guinea
centimos	guarani	Paraguay
centimos	sol	Peru
groszy	zloty	Poland
bani	leu	Rumania
centimos	dobra	São Tomé- Principe
hallalas	rial	Saudi Arabia
cents	rupee	Seychelles, Sri Lanka
cents	leone	Sierra Leone
halierov	koruna	Slovak Rep.

COINING.

stotins	tolar	Slovenia
cents	shilling	Somalia, Tanzania, Uganda
cents	rand	South Africa
centimos	peseta	Spain
piastres	pound	Sudan
cents	lilangeni	Swaziland
öre	krona	Sweden
piastres	pound	Syria
cents	yüan	Taiwan
satang	baht	Thailand
seniti	pa'anga	Tonga
kurus	lira	Turkey
pence	pound	UK
centesimos	peso	Uruguay
centimes	vatu	Vanuatu
centimos	bolivar	Venezuela
xu	dong	Vietnam
sene	tala	Western Samoa
fils	rial	Yemen
makuta	zaire	Zaire
ngwee	kwacha	Zambia

One hundred is also the number of:
pounds of oxygen in the average human body
women seduced in France by Mozart's Don Giovanni
yards in an American football field
years Sleeping Beauty slept

Films include:
Anne One Hundred (1933): romance based on a play by Sewell Collins
100 Men and a Girl (1937): musical
The Hundred-pound Window (1943): Richard Attenborough in a crime drama
100 Cries of Terror (1964): horror story based on works of Edgar Allen Poe
100 Rifles (1969): violent western with Burt Reynolds and Racquel Welch
Mama Turns a Hundred (1979): Spanish comedy with Geraldine Chaplin
100% Bonded (1987): spy film with Sean Connery

Book: *100 Days of Sodom* by the Marquis de Sade

Dodie Smith's Dalmatians
members of the Estonian parliament
metres length of one side of the square base of the Eiffel Tower

people per square mile on earth, excluding Antarctica
quatrains in Edward Fitzgerald's translation of the *Rubaiyat* of Omar
    Khayyam

Films include:
101 Dalmatians (1961): Disney feature-length cartoon
101 Problems of Hercules (1966): cartoon feature
101 Dalmatians (1996): with Glenn Close as Cruella de Vil

■ 102

is the number of films reviewed in 'Cluck – The True Story of Chickens
in The Cinema' (1981), by Jon-Stephen Fink, the definitive work for
anyone interested in films in which chickens (or in some cases their eggs)
make an appearance.

102 is also the number of:
days the average sixty-year-old male has spent shaving
days the longest recorded case of constipation lasted
floors in Empire State Building
verses in the final section of the prose Edda of Snorri Sturluson, each
    verse illustrating a different metre or stanza form

Film: *101 Boulevard Haussmann* (1991): love story based on life of
    Marcel Proust

---

119 kilometres per hour for a typhoon

■ 103

The number 103 is connected to one of the more deeply inconsequential numerological coincidences ever discovered. Among the buses that skirt the southern fringes of Greater London, the 103 goes from Rainham War Memorial to Bromley in Kent. Now if you add up the positions in the alphabet of the letters in 'Rainham War Memorial', you get 18+1+9+14+8+1+13+23+1+18+13+5+13+15+18+9+1+12 = 192, and if you do the same for Bromley you get 2+18+15+13+12+4+25 = 89. Subtract one from the other, and you get 103, the number of the bus.

103 is also the number of:
Archbishops of Canterbury
Germans expelled from Great Britain 1907-14 for soliciting or
    importuning
kilograms weight of the heaviest mountain lion on record
kilometres-per-hour wind speed required to reach storm force on the
    Beaufort scale
'nonstellar objects' – galaxies, nebulae and star clusters – listed in Charles
    Messier's catalogue in 1784
species of crows

■ 104

There were 104 columns (some say 106) in the Temple of Olympian Zeus, the largest temple ever built in Greece, begun around 530 BC and completed around AD 125. Sixteen of the columns remain today, which curiously enough is the same as the number of stones still standing at Stonehenge (→30).

104 is also the number of:
characters named John in feature films 1983-93
pilgrims who set sail to America from Plymouth in 1620
symphonies by Haydn
the Tupolev Tu-104, the Soviet Union's first twin-jet airliner, first
    produced in 1955

■ 105

Element 105 is an artificially produced radioactive element about which the Russians and Americans are constantly arguing. The Russians, who claim they produced it first, want to call it nielsbohrium, in honour of the Danish physicist Niels Bohr, but the Americans, who are convinced otherwise, propose the name hahnium, after the German chemist Otto Hahn.

105 is also the number of:
bears Davy Crockett claimed to have killed in seven months
calories in a large banana
flights made by the Wright brothers
times Billy Wright played football for England
times Shakespeare uses the word 'damned'

■ **106**

disorderly houses involved in prosecutions in England and Wales in
    1856-57
polished diamonds cut from the Cullinan – the largest diamond ever
    discovered, which was found near Pretoria, South Africa, in 1905 and
    weighed 1,306 carats
population of Ellesmere Island, off Greenland, the world's tenth largest
    island
times Bobby Charlton played football for England

■ **107**

centimetres height of
    men's high hurdles
days in the gestation
    period of a lion or tiger
essays written by Michel de Montaigne
minutes maximum duration of a lunar eclipse
people per square kilometre in Indonesia or Portugal
square kilometres in Jerusalem
verses excluded from the Biblical Book of Esther, which appear as
    Additions to the Book of Esther in the Apocrypha

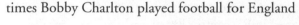

■ **108**

beads in a Tibetan rosary
gallons in a butt of ale
grams of cheese eaten by average Briton per week
pounds record weight for a marrow

minutes Yuri Gagarin was airborne

women serving jail sentences in England and Wales for robbery at the beginning of 1997

■ **109**

catches taken by Sir Garfield Sobers in Test matches

centimetres width of the Turin shroud

marches written by Edwin Franko Goldman (1878-1956)

times a year the average male has sex, according to a survey of fifteen countries conducted by *Esquire* magazine

times the diameter of the earth would fit into the diameter of the sun (which means, of course, that the volume of the sun is more than one million times that of the earth)

car-making companies in the world in 1900 (down from over 300 in 1895)

■ **110**

feet length of the longest blue whale ever measured

heads of state who gathered in Riocentro, Brazil, in June 1992 for the Earth Summit (UN Conference on Environment and Development)

men sent to prison in London between 1820 and 1824 for 'indecently exposing their persons'

pounds paid for two pairs of Queen Victoria's silk stockings at auction in 1978

storeys of both Sears Tower, Chicago and the World Trade Centre, New York

■ **111**

articles in the United Nations charter

F-111 strike aircraft, not to be confused with the FB-111, a bomber version, or the EF-111, which is described as an 'electronic countermeasure' of the same aeroplane

kilograms of moon rocks brought back on Apollo 17

kilometres between two meridians (degrees of latitude) at the equator

metres height of the Aswan High Dam

record number of beermats flipped and caught

times the Wimbledon Lawn Tennis Championships have been played

■ 112

drainage pumps in the New Orleans flood prevention system
chemical elements
feet of the highest recorded wave
mountains in Java
national lottery tickets sold every second in Britain
pounds in a hundredweight
short stories by Henry James

■ 113

days in the gestation period of a pig
kilometres to the horizon for an observer one kilometre above sea level in
    a plane or up a mountain
kinds of plum introduced by the American plant breeder
    Luther Burbank
nations in the Non-Aligned Movement

■ 114

centimetres in an ell, an old measure for cloth
chapters of the Quran
cigarettes smoked per week by the average British male smoker
Coca-Colas drunk per head in the UK in 1995
radios for every hundred people in the UK
years the Hundred Years War lasted
years in a million hours

■ 115

calories in an ounce of cheddar cheese
daily newspapers in Sweden
feet length of the ancient Greek trireme
grams of fleece produced each year by a vicuna, the smallest member of
    the camel family, with the finest fleece of any wool-bearing animal
kilometres length of the river Eure in France
living rooms in Spruce Tree House, a thirteenth-century ruin in Mesa
    Verde National Park, Colorado, built by American Indian cliff
    dwellers
marine species of angelfish
miles length of Hadrian's Wall
species of the Acer genus of tree, including sycamore and maple
species of butterflyfish

123 journalists in jail

hours it would take to play all the music composed by Purcell
people per square kilometre in Northern Ireland
poems in the only surviving manuscript of the Latin lyric poet Catullus.
    His verses tell of his love for Clodia, an aristocratic maiden whom he
    refers to as 'Lesbia'. But his passion ended in disillusionment
square kilometres in Jersey
square kilometres in Manchester

■ 117

*'Seventy minutes had passed before Mr Lloyd George arrived at his
proper theme. He spoke for a hundred and seventeen minutes, in
which period he was detected only once in the use of an argument.'*
Arnold Bennett

117 was the number of people who founded the 'Lost Colony' at
Roanoke Island, off the coast of what is now North Carolina, in 1587. It
was England's second colony in America, the first, two years earlier also
at Roanoke, having ended in the colonists giving up and returning to
England. The 117 of the new colony became 118 on 18 August 1857,
when Virginia Dare was born – the first English person born in America.
John White, the leader of the new colony, went back to England for
fresh supplies, but the war between England and Spain prevented him
from returning to America until 1590. When he arrived, the only traces
of the colonists were the letters CRO carved on one tree and the word
'Croatoan' on another. Nobody knows what happened to the 117 lost
colonists.

117 is also the number of:
the F-117 stealth fighter of the US Air Force
German scientists, including Wernher von Braun, sent to the United
    States at the end of the Second World War to work on guided missile
    systems
grammes of baked beans eaten by the average Briton each week
kilometres per hour wind speed to be exceeded for hurricane force on the
    Beaufort Scale
nations that approved the Law of the Sea Treaty in 1982
'You know's counted in a forty-five-minute radio broadcast in Los
    Angeles in 1996 by Barney Oldfield, a retired Air Force colonel

factories in Turkey in 1923
inches length of the Willamette meteorite, found in the Willamette
    Valley, Oregon – the largest meteorite ever found in the United States
people per sq km in Albania and Armenia
pieces into which the 'Winged Victory' statue of Nike, the goddess of
    victory, was broken when it was found in 1863. It dates back to about
    180 BC and is now in the Louvre.
Test matches played by Graham Gooch

airports in Algeria
caps for Northern Ireland's football team won by Pat Jennings
kilometres per hour at which a cyclone is called a typhoon
square kilometres in Dublin
square kilometres in Ottawa

hours it would take to play all the music composed by Beethoven
kilometres the furthest you can be from the sea in Great Britain
maximum number of cardinals in the College to elect a Pope
members of the Knesset, the Israeli parliament
members of the National Assembly of Senegal

horse-race winners ridden by Fred Winter in the 1952-53 season
Methodist preachers in the UK in 1770
points to win at cribbage
sexual partners of ancient kings of China: one queen, three consorts, nine
    wives of second rank, twenty-seven wives of third rank, eighty-one
    concubines

consecutive victories by Ed Moses in 400m hurdles
different type-faces designed by Frederic William Goudy (1865-1947)
metres height of the Lighthouse of Alexandria, one of the Seven
    Wonders of the Ancient World
people killed in the floods caused by Hurricane Agnes in 1972

125 calories in a large apple

persons on board the *Dunbar* when she was wrecked on the rocks at
Sydney harbour in 1859. Only one survived
square kilometres of St Helena

■ **123**

fables by the third-century Roman author Babrius
journalists in jail for their professional activities at the beginning of 1993
years to which Aaron lived in the Old Testament

Two films have this number in the title:
The Taking of Pelham 123 (1974): hostage drama with Walter Matthau
    and Robert Shaw based on the novel by John Godey
123 Monster Express (1977): murders and a bomb on a bus in Thailand

■ **124**

Japanese emperors in an unbroken line from the same family
kilometres length of the coastline of Benin
pounds record weight for a pumpkin

people per square mile in New Hampshire

■ **125**

baryton trios composed by Haydn (his patron Prince Nicholas of
    Esterhazy played the baryton)
calories in a large raw apple
cruising speed of an Intercity-125 train
plays written by Dion Boucicault (1820-90), an Irish-American actor-
    manager
Test matches played by Sunil Gavaskar
years, from 1835-1960, for which Rio de Janeiro was Brazil's capital

Film: *125 Rooms of Comfort* (1974): horror and madness

126 gallons in a butt of wine

*'This note doth tell me of ten thousand French
That in the field lie slain; of princes in this number,
And nobles bearing banners, there lie dead
One hundred twenty-six.'*
William Shakespeare, *Henry V,* 1599

126 is the number of:
centuries scored by W. G. Grace in first-class cricket
characters named Jack in feature films 1983-93
gallons in a butt of wine
people per square kilometre in Andorra and Tonga
score for Quartzy played as an opening move in Scrabble

■ 127

hottest temperature on the moon in degrees Celsius
LZ-127 Graf Zeppelin, the most successful rigid airship ever built
recorded ways of spelling the surname Raleigh; Sir Walter Raleigh
   himself is known to have spelt his name as Rawleyghe, Rawley and
   Ralegh, while his colleagues and friends used Ralo, Ralle, Raulie,
   Rawlegh, Rawlighe, Rawlye and more than sixty other variants. The
   one they never seem to have used is Raleigh, which became the
   dominant spelling through other people of the same name.
years to which Sarah, Abraham's wife, lived in the Old Testament

■ 128

Americans killed when the *Lusitania* was sunk in 1915 (→1,198)
cubic feet in a cord – a unit for measuring firewood
metres length of Count Ferdinand von Zeppelin's first airship
members in the Mexican senate or Lebanon's National Assembly

■ 129

kilometres per hour top speed of an osprey
metres height of Montmartre, the tallest hill in Paris
mystery novels by Erle Stanley Gardner (→82)
nominations for the 1997 Nobel Peace Prize
people per square mile in Belarus

'If Mr Perry can tell me how to convey a wife and five children a distance of a hundred and thirty miles with no greater expense or inconvenience than a distance of forty, I would be as willing to prefer Cromer to Southend as he could himself.'
Jane Austen, *Emma*, 1816

130 is the number of:
different names for the oak tree in American dialects
lynchings in the US in 1901
test-tube babies born in Australia in 1984 (first year of such)
words in Chambers Dictionary ending in 'lessness'

■ 131

national scout organisations within the World Organisation of the Scout
    Movement
people killed in the 1964 earthquake that hit Alaska
skyscrapers in New York

■ 132

Germans captured by Sgt Alvin York at Battle of the Argonne,
    8 October 1918
islands of Hawaii
rooms in the White House

■ 133

common councilmen of the Corporation of the City of London
highest number sharing jackpot in UK Lottery
Indian tribes recognised in Mexico in 1914
poems in Tennyson's *In Memoriam*

■ 134

countries represented at the World Health Organisation conference in
    Alma-Ata, Kazakhstan, in 1978, which declared the goal of 'Health
    for All' by the year 2000
hours of music composed by Schubert
metres above sea level of the top of the arch of Sydney Harbour Bridge

■ 135

grams of biscuits eaten by the average Briton each week
grams of breakfast cereal eaten by average Briton each week
times the words 'read my lips' appeared in the *Washington Post* in the
first two years of the Bush Presidency

■ 136

*'In the spring I have counted one hundred and thirty-six different
kinds of weather inside twenty-four hours.'*
Mark Twain, Speech to New England Society, 1886

136 is the number of:
Fahrenheit degrees of highest temperature ever recorded – in the Libyan
desert
grams of sugar eaten by the average Briton each week
marches written by John Philip Sousa
standard tiles in a mah-jongg set

■ 137

Celsius degrees of the boiling point of acetic anhydride ($CH_3CO_2)O$
deaths caused by Atlantic hurricanes in 1995
internal diameter of the dome of St Peter's in Rome in feet
height in metres of the Old Man of Hoy in the Orkney islands

F. Schubert

degrees Celsius to which milk is heated for a few seconds in the process called 'ultrapasteurisation'
length of the winning world record throw, in feet, by Dewy Bartlett (ex-governor of Oklahoma), in the 1972 world cow-pat throwing championships
population of Weston-super-Mare in 1801
references to goat or goats in the Bible
members of the National Assembly of Madagascar

length of the River Dee, in kilometres, from the Cairngorms to Aberdeen
years of age of Herbert Badgery, the confidence trickster in Peter Carey's novel *Illywhacker*

beats per minute of a foetal heart
bottles of wine drunk annually in France per capita
skeins in a bundle

countries reporting no cases of polio in 1993
days a new-born grey-headed albatross stays in the nest
kilometres of the longest Roman aqueduct – in Carthage

books in Livy's History of Rome, of which only thirty-five survive
people killed in the Durban riots of 1949
pictures by François Lemoyne on the vault of the Salon d'Hercule at Versailles

diameter of the Pantheon in Rome in feet
grammes of fish products eaten by the average Briton each week
Oxford-Cambridge boat races between 1829 and 1997
square kilometres of Lake Garda, the largest lake in Italy
volumes Balzac planned for his La Comédie Humaine – of which he completed eighty

■ 144

a gross
murders in London in 1996
nuclear warheads under British control in February 1993

■ 145

kilometres per hour top speed of a bobsleigh
length of Amiens Cathedral in metres
area of Lake Como in Italy in square kilometres
area of Pittsburgh in square kilometres

■ 146

British prisoners thrown into the 'Black Hole of Calcutta' on 20 June
    1756. According to legend, only twenty-three survived, but more
    reputable research puts the number of dead at only forty-three
neutrons in the heaviest isotope of uranium

■ 147

average annual rainfall in Rwanda in centimetres
horserace winners ridden by Fred Archer in 1874
maximum break in snooker
original height of the Great Pyramid of Khufu in metres
punches landed by Jimmy Carruthers in the 2 minutes 19 seconds it
    took him to win the world bantamweight championship from
    Vic Toweel in 1952

■ 148

length of the coastline of Dominica in kilometres
members of the House of Representatives in Australia
Mormon settlers led by Brigham Young to Utah in 1847
tornadoes in 24 hours in the USA, 3rd-4th April 1974

■ 149

degrees Celsius to which milk is heated for UHT (ultra high
    temperature) pasteurisation
doctors per 100,000 people in Brazil
languages spoken in the old USSR
small islands in the Bay of Islands off the north tip of New Zealand

131 skyscrapers in New York

■ 150

'And the waters prevailed upon the earth an hundred and fifty days.'
Genesis 7:24)

150 is the number of:
days in the gestation period of a goat or sheep
French expelled from Great Britain between 1907 and 1914 for soliciting
  or importuning
mentions of asses in the Bible
places called Newton in the UK
psalms in the Bible
wigs owned by Queen Elizabeth I

■ 151

the average depth of the Java Sea in feet
the final psalm, included in the apocrypha of the Greek Orthodox Bible
length in miles of the Arno river in Italy
people per square kilometre in Lithuania
performing artists in the US listed as having communist associations by
  investigators for Senator McCarthy in 1950

■ 152

height of a badminton net at its centre in centimetres
minutes Neil Armstrong spent on the moon
references to bullocks in the Bible
runs scored by W. G. Grace at the Oval in 1880 – the first English Test
  match century

■ 153

John 21:11 refers to the 153 fishes caught by Christ's disciples, though
the significance of the number has never been properly established. One
theory holds that if you add the Ten Commandments to the Seven Gifts
of the Holy Spirit, you get seventeen, and 153 is the sum of the integers
from 1 to 17, but this sounds a little fishy.

153 is also the number of:
pieces for piano in Bela Bartok's 'Microkosmos'
area of Minneapolis or the British Virgin Islands in square kilometres
times round the world all the roads in America would go

days it would take a spacecraft to reach the sun, travelling at a constant
   speed of 40,200 kilometres per hour, which is the speed needed to
   escape the earth's gravity
the closest Ernest Shackleton came to the South Pole in his 1908
   expedition in kilometres
people per square mile in Indiana
sonnets by William Shakespeare (though there is some doubt about the
   authorship of the last two)

length in kilometres of the London sewerage system designed by Joseph
   Bazalgette in 1865
medical schools in the US and Canada in 1910
members of the Storting – the Norwegian parliament
depth in metres below sea level of the lowest point in Africa
miles per hour that is the maximum speed of a human body in free fall
miles per second at which the sun revolves around the centre of the
   galaxy
newspaper chains in the US
area of Christmas Island in the Indian Ocean in square kilometres
area of Staten Island, NY City, in square kilometres
tribes belonging to the National Congress of American Indians

consecutive weeks for which Ivan Lendl was ranked the world's number
    one tennis player
fairy tales by Hans Anderson
metres length of Westminster Abbey
Test matches played by Allan Border

height in centimetres of Maureen (Little Mo) Connolly, who became the
    first woman to complete a Grand Slam in tennis in 1953
height in centimetres of Napoleon I – about average for a Frenchman at
    the time, though most high-ranking soldiers and statesmen were taller
maximum depth in feet of the Sea of Galilee
height in metres of the spires of Cologne Cathedral
people per square mile in the Seychelles
professional tennis singles titles won by Chris Evert

height in metres of Blackpool tower
length in metres of Milan Cathedral
unions affiliated to the Australian Council of Trade Unions
verses in the Greek national anthem

■ 159

'In Perthshire, the idiots are two hundred and eight, the lunatics only one hundred and fifty-nine.'
Sir A. Halliday, 1828

159 is the number of:
days' holiday a year the ancient Romans enjoyed under the Emperor
    Claudius
litres in a barrel of oil
vessels in the Japanese Navy in February 1993

■ 160

men needed to move the body of Jumbo the elephant from the tracks in
    Ontario in September 1885 after he was killed in a railway accident.
    This was the original Jumbo, after whom all later elephants,
    aeroplanes and gigantic special offers were named
perches in an acre
number of the White House in Pennsylvania Avenue
seconds for the fastest haircut: as performed by Trevor Mitchell of
    Southampton on 28 October 1996

■ 161

length of the coastline of Mauritius in kilometres
new bishops named by the Vatican in 1996
vessels (including submarines) in the Royal Navy in February 1993

■ 162

height of Arc de Triomph de L'Etoile, in feet
cells in the brain of the intestinal worm, Ascaris

■ 163

The Messerschmitt Me 163 rocket-powered plane was developed by
Germany in the early years of the Second World War. It was capable of
speeds of almost 1,000 kilometres per hour and was the prototype for the
Me 163 Komet which flew combat missions late in the war.

163 is the number of:
states with which the Vatican has full diplomatic ties
villages wiped out when Krakatoa erupted in 1883

■ **164**

poems in *The Temple* (1633) by George Herbert. He also wrote the well-
    known hymn 'Let all the world in every corner sing'
references to horses in the Bible

■ **165**

beads in a rosary (15 sets of ten 'Hail Mary's' each separated by a Lord's
    Prayer)
curtain calls received by Luciano Pavarotti at the Berlin Opera on
    24 February 1988
references to rams in the Bible

■ **166**

members of the Dail Eireann, the Irish parliament
people injured in train accidents in Britain in the year 1995-96
references to ox or oxen in the Bible

■ **167**

countries in which Rotary International operates
height in feet of the planned 'world's tallest Jesus' statue in Troina, Sicily
letters in the official name of Bangkok: Krung thep mahanakhon bovorn
    ratanakosin mahintharayutthaya mahadilok pop noparatratchathani
    burirom udomratchanivetma hasathan amornpiman avatarnsa thit
    sakkathattiyavisnukarmprasit
people killed in the Piper Alpha oil rig disaster in 1988
tennis singles titles won by Martina Navratilova

■ **168**

metres height of the Grand Coulee dam across the Columbia River
people killed by the Oklahoma City bomb in 1995
people per square kilometre in Switzerland
razor blades sold by Gillette in their first year
square kilometres per television set in Chad

---

136 degrees Fahrenheit in the Libyan desert

amendments to the constitution of Nevada
length in kilometres of the Suez Canal
miles of railroad in Luxembourg
municipalities in Cuba
towns in Connecticut

metres length of Winchester Cathedral, the longest church in England
millimetres length of the standard European condom, according to the
    1996 European standard EN600 – an increase of about 2 mm on the
    previous average length
oarsmen in the crew of a trireme (sixty-two thranite, fifty-four zygiah,
    fifty-four thalamian oars)
people who travelled with Henry Ford, and at his expense, to Europe in
    1915 to try to persuade the warring nations to seek peace
square metres of floor space occupied by ENIAC, the first electronic
    computer, built in 1946

Gamma Virginis, also called Porrima, in the constellation of Virgo,
    consists of a pair of fourth-magnitude yellow stars that orbit each
    other every 171 years.
    171 is also the length in kilometres of the Suez Canal and the number
of murders in London in 1995.

countries that competed in the Barcelona '92 Olympics
miles per hour of the highest wind speed ever recorded in Britain – in the
    Cairngorms on 20 March 1986
pounds of potatoes eaten per head each year in the UK

height in centimetres of a Shire horse
degrees of frost on the moon in the coldest part of the night
environmental treaties recorded in the Worldwatch 'Vital Signs 1995'
    report
institutes of higher education in Illinois
metres above sea level of Yding Skovhoj, the highest point in Denmark

■ 174

British wounded (and seventy-three killed) at the battle of Lexington, the
    opening battle of the American revolution
pounds weight of the largest marlin ever caught
square kilometres of Washington DC

■ 175

age to which Abraham lived in the Bible
countries represented when Nelson Mandela was inaugurated as South
    African president on 10 May 1994
days gestation period of a sheep
professional fights won by Sugar Ray Robinson (from a total of 202)
hours music composed by J. S. Bach
metres depth of the Meteor Crater in Arizona, believed to have been
    formed about 50,000 years ago by the impact of an iron meteorite
    weighing 300,000 metric tons
pairs of legs of the leggiest centipede

■ 176

earth days for one day on Mercury
grammes of bananas eaten by the average Briton each week
references to lions in the Bible

■ 177

days the Roman Games lasted in the middle of the fourth century – ten
    days of gladiators, sixty-six of chariot races, 101 of theatrical
    performances
kilometres of railway in Borneo
Russians and Poles expelled from Great Britain 1906-14 for larceny and
    receiving

■ 178

sesame seeds in the average Big Mac bun, according to Ray Croc
gold medals won by the UK in the Olympics altogether
vehicles registered to the Russian UN mission in New York

---

138 references to goats in the Bible

elected members of the Folketing, the Danish parliament
languages of the Indian sub-continent described in George Grierson's
    Linguistic Survey of India 1903-18
species of trees counted in a one hectare area of tropical rain forest in
    South America
area of Washington DC in square kilometres

degrees in an about-turn
top score with three darts
white stones in a game of Go

feet length of the Reclining Buddha in Pegu, Burma
members of the United Nations at the end of 1993
professional fights won by Henry 'Homicide Hank' Armstrong, the only
    boxer to hold world titles at three weights simultaneously
area of Brooklyn in square kilometres
black stones in a game of Go

ball-boys and ball-girls on duty at Wimbledon 1997
couples married at Bangrak registry office in Thailand on St Valentine's
    Day 1995 – the name means 'village of love'
members of the Belgian senate
VCs awarded in World War II

degrees below zero for the boiling point of liquid oxygen
elected members of the Nationalrat of Austria
grams of apples eaten by average Briton each week
length in miles of the Aara river, the longest in Switzerland
parishes in Iceland
shells from the *Kaiser Wilhelm Geschutz* ('Paris gun') that landed within
    the boundaries of the city of Paris in 1918

■ 184

Norwegians voted against independence from Sweden in 1905
people killed by Hurricane Diana in 1955
area of Belgrade in square kilometres

■ 185

defendants in the Nuremberg trials from 1946-49
length in feet of the Sphinx
members of the United Nations
weight in pounds of Sputnik 1, the first ever artificial satellite, launched
    in 1957
species of the order Artiodactyla, the even-toed ungulates

■ 186

diameter in kilometres of Himalia, a small satellite of Jupiter
record distance in feet that a wellington boot has been thrown

■ 187

defenders of the Alamo in 1836
height in feet of the Taj Mahal above its platform

islands in Franz Josef Land in the Barents Sea – the northernmost part of
    Russia
length in kilometres of the River Forth
length in metres of the Colosseum in Rome

■ 188

centimetres of rain that fell in twenty-four hours on Cilaos, on the island
    of Reunion, in the Indian Ocean during 15-16 March 1952, the
    highest rainfall ever recorded for a twenty-four hour period
kilometres into space travelled by Alan Shepard, the first American in
    space, on 5 May 1961
passengers, on average, on a non-local train in Britain
references to lambs in the Bible

■ 189

carved memorial stones on the Washington Monument
kilometres of underground tunnels on the Paris Metro
litres in one barrel of alcohol
stairs to the top of the pedestal of the Statue of Liberty
wickets taken in Test matches by Sidney Francis Barnes (1873-1967)

■ 190

average weight in kilograms of an Indian tiger
daily newspapers in Argentina
litres of blood filtered each day by the kidneys
pony express stations in the US in 1860

■ 191

bedrooms in Claridge's (→53)
centimetres maximum permitted cue length in a game of shuffleboard

■ 192

independent countries in the world in 1995
metres height of the gateway arch in St Louis
places called Fairway in US

■ 193

'There are one hundred and ninety-three living species of monkeys and apes. One hundred and ninety-two of them are covered with hair. The exception is a naked ape self-named Homo sapiens.'
Desmond Morris, *The Naked Ape*, 1967

193 is the number of:
height in centimetres of Charles de Gaulle
centimetres of snow that fell at Silver Lake, Colorado, in twenty-four
    hours on 14-15 April 1921, the heaviest snowfall ever recorded
length in kilometres of Long Island, New York
lives lost when the *Herald of Free Enterprise* sank off Zeebrugge in 1987

■ 194

different meanings of 'set' listed in the *OED*
films in which Mary Pickford appeared

■ 195

countries where Coca-Cola is sold
square kilometres of the Channel Islands

■ 196

degrees below zero at which nitrogen liquifies
wingspan in feet of the Boeing 747 Jumbo jet. This is roughly 75 feet
    longer than the first ever flight by airplane made by Orville Wright in
    1903

■ 197

centuries scored in his career by Sir Jack Hobbs
countries competing in the Atlanta Olympics in 1996

■ 198

people per square mile in Turkey

■ 199

days in office of President James Garfield in 1881
executions in the US in 1935

■ 200

grammes of frozen vegetables eaten by the average Briton each week
mentions of sheep in the Bible
pounds (or dollars) for passing Go in Monopoly

Film: *200 Motels* (1971): Ringo Starr in the life and times of
    Frank Zappa

■ 201

length in kilometres of the South Esk River, the longest river in
    Tasmania
miles length of the river Clutha, the longest river in New Zealand's
    South Island
T1-201, a radio-active isotope of thallium that is useful in diagnosing
    certain types of heart disease

■ 202

animal and plant sanctuaries in India
hours of music composed by Mozart

■ 203

canons in the 'General Norms' of the Code of Canon Law
inhabited islands in the Maldives (→1,196)
members of the House of Representatives in Pennsylvania
miles above the earth, the maximum reached by Yuri Gagarin in 1961
miles from the surface of Mars that was the nearest the Mariner
    spacecraft reached in 1975
square miles in Bucharest
square miles in Budapest
years between James Madison's drafting the 27th Amendment in 1789
    and the US Congress ratifying it in 1992

days it took William Willis to sail from Peru to Australia (with a stop in Samoa for repairs) on a steel pontoon raft in 1963-64

islands in the Andaman group in the Bay of Bengal. The capital, Port Blair, is the only town

length in kilometres of the longest fjord in Norway. Thanks to all the fjords – narrow inlets of the sea – the total length of the coast is about 21,350 km, which is about half the distance round the world

weight in metric tons of the Statue of Liberty

parliamentary penises Lindi StClair claimed to have known in twenty years of business

■ **205**

bones of a horse

square kilometres of Cincinnati or Osaka

■ **206**

bones in an adult human body

marines guarding the 759 criminals on board the first convict ships to Australia

■ **207**

largest number of people ever carried in an airship
places called Midway in the US
television broadcast stations in the UK

■ **208**

feet height of the Cape Hatteras lighthouse in North Carolina, the tallest
    in the US
idiots in Perthshire in 1828 according to Sir A. Halliday (→159)
length in kilometres of the River Wye
people per square kilometre in Malawi
square miles of Guam in the Western Pacific

■ **209**

stamps stuck on envelopes in five minutes by Dean Gould of Felixtowe
    to set a new record in 1997

■ **210**

people per doctor in Italy – the world's most doctor-rich country
width in mm of A4 paper
'210 Coca-Cola Bottles' by Andy Warhol (sold for $1.9m in 1992)

■ **211**

days Valentin Lebedev remained in space aboard Salyut 7 in 1982-83
length in metres of the *Great Eastern*, designed by Isambard Kingdom
    Brunel, which remained the longest ship in the world for 40 years
    from its launch in 1858

■ **212**

boiling point of water in degrees Fahrenheit. His temperature scale set
    the freezing point of salt water at zero, and the human blood
    temperature supposedly at 100, which suggests that he was running a
    slight temperature that day
members of the Belgian Chamber of Representatives

■ **214**

Batman articles on sale in 1989
meanings of the word 'ka' in Japanese

215

daily newspapers published in Belarus
area of Cairo or Newcastle in square kilometres

218

grains in the weight of a biblical shekel

220

yards in a furlong

221

passengers killed in crashes on British airlines 1970-79

222

offences punishable by death in GB in 1819

224

minutes the average Brazilian spends each year making international
phone calls

225

earth days in year of Venus
grams of fresh green vegetables eaten each week by the average Briton

226

length in feet of the 'Long Man' of Wilmington, East Sussex

227

ways of cooking chicken in Escoffier's 'Guide Culinaire' 4th edition
(1921)

228

American slang terms for drunkenness listed by Benjamin Franklin in
1737

229

people found guilty of murder in England and Wales between 1805 and 1818

Xerox copies made on average for each of the 35,000 delegates to the UN Women's Conference in Peking in 1996

230

lynchings in US in 1892, the record for a calendar year

231

'Pacific 231' is a 'symphonic movement' by Arthur Honneger. Naming his work after an American railway engine, the Swiss composer said: 'I have not aimed to imitate the noise of an engine, but rather to express in terms of music a visual impression and physical enjoyment.'

231 is also the number of:
years the Lord Chancellor acted as official censor of plays (1737-1968)
women in Germany seduced by Mozart's Don Giovanni

234

men arrested in Paris in 1749 for homosexuality

235

isotope of uranium used in making an atom bomb

236

people per square mile in the UK

237

grams of poultry eaten each week by the average Briton

239

sled dogs in harness that pulled a 12.5 ton truck 50 metres on 10 September 1995 to set a new record
area of Singapore in square miles

■ **240**

people per square kilometre in the UK

Film: *240-Robert* (1979): plane crash suspense

■ **243**

days in the rotation period of Venus, which, like Uranus, rotates about
its axis in the opposite direction to its rotation about the sun.

■ **244**

miles length of the Mason-Dixon line, drawn by Charles Mason and
Jeremiah Dixon in 1763 to settle a border dispute between
Pennsylvania and Maryland
trespassers or suicides killed by trains in Britain in the year 1995-96

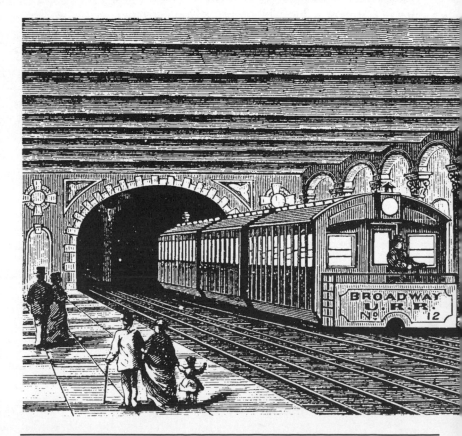

■ **246**

'It was the business of the All-British Company to produce seventeen exceptionally bad and cheap films every year in England in order to allow two hundred and forty-six exceptionally bad and expensive films to be imported every year into England from Hollywood. This is called the Quota System.'
A. G. MacDonnell, *How Like an Angel,* 1934

246 is also the number of people killed by hailstones in Moradabad, N. India in a storm in 1880.

■ **247**

wing-flaps per second of a bee

■ **249**

miles on the New York subway system

250

hedgehogs to equal the weight of one lion

251

miles on the London Underground network
people killed in the earthquake in Yunnan, China, on 3 February 1996

253

people you need to encounter to have a greater than even chance of
meeting one who shares your birthday

255

names in first phone book produced by the London Telephone
Company

256

acres in a hide (a twelfth-century land measure)
cycles per second of middle C
tambourines played in 20.47 seconds by Rowdy Blackwell on 28
October 1996 in a record-breaking performance for charity

260

days in the Aztec religious calendar

261

bastards born in Rochdale, Lancashire, 1661-1720

265

people per square mile in Pennsylvania

266

average number of days from conception to birth of a human being
stations on the London underground

267

lowest four-round total in the British Open Golf Championship as
  scored by Greg Norman in 1993

268

'Two hundred and sixty-eight sequins are more than I dare lay out.'
Horace Walpole, 1759

268 is also the number of words in the Gettysburg Address.

270

record score in the US Masters Golf Championship set by Tiger Woods
  in 1997

273

diameter in miles of asteroid Hektor, the biggest discovered this century
seconds of silence in John Cage's composition '4 min 33 sec'
people per square kilometre in Israel

274

average walking speed of a woman in feet per minute

275

average walking speed of a man in feet per minute

276

murders in Dallas, Texas in 1995
breeds of bird in the Faeroe Islands

277

atomic mass of the element with atomic number 112, the heaviest ever.
  One atom was created in 1996 and lasted a third of a millisecond

279

words in the Ten Commandments in German
convicts on board the last British convict ship to dock in Australia in
1868

280

cities with more than one million people at the beginning of 1997

282

members of the Canadian House of Commons

285

participants in 1896 Olympics

286

verses in chapter two of the Quran, its longest chapter

288

gallons in a chaldron

290

women serving jail sentences in England and Wales at the start of 1997
for violence against the person

292

offensive epigrams written by John Davies (1565?-1618), a poet and
writing-master of Hereford. His comments on his contemporaries
were described as 'scoundrelisms' by F. E. Hulme in 1902.

297

length in mm of A4 paper

■ 299

pairs of size 12 Bruno Magli shoes ever sold – as seen at the trial of O. J. Simpson

■ 300

golden bees found in the tomb of Childeric, an eighth century king of the Merovingians

Films include:
The 300 Spartans (1962): re-enactment of the Battle of Thermopylae in 480 BC
The 300 Year Weekend (1971): drama

■ 302

escalators on the London underground

■ 303

hours it would take to play all the music composed by Handel
deposits lost by the Natural Law Party in the 1992 British general election

■ 305

lightbulbs on the clock above Times Square registering the US national debt
mentions of 'wilderness' in the Revised Standard Bible

■ 312

'One out of three hundred and twelve Americans is a bore, for instance, and a healthy male adult bore consumes each year one and a half times his own weight in other people's patience.'
John Updike, *Assorted Prose* (1965) 'Confessions of a Wild Bore'

312 is also the number of sports-related riots in the US between 1960 and 1972.

315

bombs dropped on Germany in World War II for every bomb that fell
    on Britain
days in the gestation period of a camel

317

length in kilometres of the average domestic flight by a UK airline
    (→1,032)

Film: *317th Platoon* (1965): French anti-war film about Vietnam

318

times the mass of the Earth to equal that of Jupiter

319

pencil-makers in Great Britain at the time of the 1851 census

■ **321**

kilometres a year walked by the average Briton

325

albums in George V's stamp collection
miles travelled each year by train by the average Briton

327

words a minute spoken by J. F. Kennedy in a speech in 1961

329

feet height of a Coast Douglas fir in Coos County, Oregon – the tallest
    tree in the US

330

Minke whales killed by Japan in 1990

336

gestation period of a horse in days

340

days in the gestation period of a llama
hours it would take to play all the music composed by Haydn, the most
    prolific of the major composers
sheep per person in the Falkland Islands

341

suicides from the Eiffel Tower in its first 75 years

343

Coca-Colas drunk per head in the US in 1995

349

languages the entire Bible has been translated into
record number of pancake tosses in two minutes

■ **352**

days in the gestation period of a badger

353

farms in Wales affected by the Chernobyl disaster
triremes in the Ionian Greek fleet at the battle of Miletus in 499 BC
    (→170)

357

pawnbrokers' shops in Thailand

Film: *357 Magnum* (1977): murder, robbery and espionage

155 kilometres of London sewers

■ 360

degrees in a circle
different plants eaten by Santa's reindeer according to the official Santa
  in Lapland – but they don't eat carrots

■ 364

alleged number of illegitimate children of Friedrich August I of Saxony
  (King Augustus II of Poland)
total number of presents received in the song: Twelve Days of Christmas

■ 365

Best known as the number of days in a non-leap year. The ancient
Babylonians knew that, but a more accurate calendar had to wait for
Julius Caesar, who first introduced the idea of leap years to compensate
for the fact that the earth's orbit round the sun takes not 365 but
365.2422 days. The Christian church adopted the Julian calendar at the
council of Nicaea in AD 325. The next correction came in 1582 from
Pope Gregory's mathematicians and astronomers who calculated the
present system of omitting the leap day in century years, except when the
new century is divisible by four. (So 1800 and 1900 were not leap years,
but 2000 will be.) The new system guaranteed 146,097 days every 400
years, which works out at an average 365.2425 days a year. Despite the
accuracy of that figure, it took Britain another 170 years to agree to it.
And there were still many 'Give us back our eleven days' protests about
the dates that had to be dropped to make up for having had the wrong
calendar since AD 325.

365 is also the number of:
days gestation of an ass
steps leading to the top of St Paul's Cathedral
years lived by Enoch in Genesis

Film: *365 Nights in Hollywood* (1934): comedy thriller

■ 366

days in a leap year
height in feet of the dome of St Paul's Cathedral

368

security guards and commissionaires employed at the Wimbledon Lawn
  Tennis Championships in 1997

370

different cheeses in France (cited by de Gaulle as the reason the country
  could not be governed)
dollars per person per year in the gross national product of Haiti

375

asteroids discovered by K. Reinmuth of Heidelberg
runs scored by Brian Lara in a single innings playing for the West Indies
  v England, Antigua 1993-94, the highest individual innings in a Test
  match

■ **379**

black spots on Moroccan roads – at each of which at least ten accidents
  and ten deaths or serious injuries have occurred within five years

380

stones on which the Chinese calligrapher Chen Zhaoguo carved the Bible
  between 1985 and 1995. It needs magnification fifteen times to be
  legible

394

height in feet of the Buddha statue in Tokyo

398

recorded injuries connected with toilet seats in the UK in 1993

400

Film: *The 400 Blows* (1959): François Truffaut's first feature film

404

number of ways Brightlingsea has been spelt since its Celtic origin of Brictrich

413

beds owned by Louis XIV

420

people per doctor in the USA
most kittens produced by one female cat

427

record number of two-egg omelettes made in 30 minutes

432

pints in a hogshead

434

Test wickets taken by Kapil Dev, the record for any bowler

435

members of the House of Representatives in the United States
television sets per 1,000 people in the UK
vasectomies performed in a six-month period, from March to September 1995 in Iran

440

cycles per second for concert pitch A above middle C following an international agreement in 1939

442

airports in Australia

449

people killed in earthquakes throughout the world in 1996

450

pet cemeteries in the US

451

Fahrenheit 451 by Ray Bradbury – the novel's title comes from the temperature at which paper catches fire
seconds a solar eclipse may last

452

asteroids identified in the nineteenth century

■ 453

area of Andorra in square kilometres

464

the lowest temperature on Venus in degrees Celsius

466

height in feet of spire of Strasbourg Cathedral – the tallest structure in France apart from the Eiffel Tower

468

average annual rainfall in inches at Mawsynram, India, a strong candidate for the title of the wettest place on earth

469

stations on the New York subway

471

weeks in the UK charts for 'Bat Out of Hell' by Meatloaf

472

beaches in the UK

483

cinemas in Great Britain

488

average number of beans in a standard Heinz tin (→494)

491

Film: *491* (1963): Swedish teenage drama

494

average number of beans in a Tesco tin (made by Heinz) (→488)

500

sheets in a ream
Indianapolis 500

Film: *The 500 Pound Jerk* (1972): US Olympic weightlifter falls in love
with Russian gymnast

501

score required to win a leg at darts

503

pounds spent per visit to Britain by the average tourist
metres span of the Sydney Harbour Bridge

520

cells in Pentonville prison when it was built in the 1840s

530

cubic feet of air used in a day's breathing by one person

533

patented inventions of Edwin Land, inventor of the Polaroid Camera

555

feet length of St Paul's Cathedral

563

feet high statue of Chief Crazy Horse by Korczak Ziolkowski at
Thunderhead Mountain, S. Dakota

565

days a female bedbug can go without food

574

bottles of claret William Pitt the Younger is said to have drunk in a single
year (→854)

575

*'Phileas Fogg, having shut the door of his house at half-past eleven, and
having put his right foot before his left five hundred and seventy-five
times, and his left foot before his right five hundred and seventy-six
times, reached the Reform Club.'*
Jules Verne, *Around the World in Eighty Days*

576

dots on a computer screen needed to make all the Japanese characters
(→35)

577

lynchings in Mississippi 1882-1956
stairs in the annual 'Supra Ultra Stairs Climbing' event up the Fukuoka
Tower in Japan

579

years it took to build Milan cathedral

582

miles diameter of Ceres, the largest known asteroid

583

dollars per capita spent each year on defence in the UK (→1,074)

587

wing flaps per second of a mosquito

594

miles walked each year by the average housewife in the course of her duties

600

ways to make love, according to the Marquis de Sade
minimum weight of women's javelin in grams

618

caravans in Freemont, California

619

area of Singapore in square kilometres

621

faulty 'proofs' of Fermat's Last Theorem submitted in first year of the Wolfskehl Prize in 1908. The prize, for a proof of the conjecture that the equation $x^n+y^n = z^n$ cannot be satisfied for any integers, x, y, z and n, with n>2, was offered by a man whose fascination with the problem had saved him from suicide. It was finally won in 1997 by the English mathematician Andrew Wiles.

632

species officially listed as endangered in the first 20 years of the
Endangered Species Act (1973-93)

633

Film: *633 Squadron* (1964): twelve RAF Mosquito pilots bomb a
Norwegian cliff to destroy a Nazi munitions factory on a fjord.

634

VCs awarded in World War I

639

named muscles in human body

■ 640

acres in a square mile
oilwell fires in Kuwait at the end of the Gulf War

641

an important number in mathematics. Pierre Fermat, the greatest of
seventeenth century mathematicians, noticed that two plus one, and two-
squared plus one, and two-to-the-fourth plus one, and two-to-the-eighth
plus one (3, 5, 17 and 257) were all prime numbers. He conjectured that
all numbers of the same form – two raised to a power of two and one
added to the answer – were prime. This was disproved by Leonard Euler,
who found that $2^{64}+1$ (a number with nineteen digits) is divisible by
641.

650

maximum voltage of an electric eel

659

seats in the House of Commons

■ 660

gestation days of an African elephant

■ 666

'Here is wisdom. Let him that hath understanding count the number of the beast: for it is the number of a man; and his number is Six hundred threescore and six.'
The Revelation of St John the Divine, 13:18

Perhaps the strangest thing about 666 being the number of the beast is its connection with the other number of Life, the Universe and Everything, 42. The link is made in Tolstoy's *War and Peace* when Pierre reveals a secret revealed to him by 'one of his brother Masons'. A few verses earlier than that quotation from Revelation we read: *'And there was given to him a mouth speaking great things and blasphemies; and power was given to him to continue forty and two months.'* Now if we write out twenty-five letters of the alphabet (our twenty-six with 'i' and 'j' identified), then assign the numbers 1-9 to the letters a-i, then go up in tens from k (=10) to z (=160), when you add up the letters of 'L' Empereur Napoleon', you end up with the number 666. *'Moreover, by applying the same system to the words "quarante-deux", which was the term allowed to the beast that "spoke great things and blasphemies", the same number 666 was obtained; from which it follows that the limit fixed for Napoleon's power had come in the year 1812 when the French emperor was 42.'*

Macaulay, however, refused to accept this, or other equally ingenious, ways of pinning the number 666 on Napoleon. He preferred to associate the House of Commons with the Beast, because it had 658 members, three clerks, a sergeant and his deputy, a chaplain, a doorkeeper and a librarian, making a total of 666.

In 1995, hundreds of Rumanian peasants refused free shares in newly privatised industries because their serial numbers began with 666.

666 is also the average number of rolls of lavatory paper used each day in the White House.

■ 670

Martian days in a Martian year (more precisely, it is 669.774)

673

men in the Charge of the Light Brigade

675

pieces of music written by Mozart

677

homicides in England and Wales in 1994

678

area of Bahrain in square kilometres

679

square centimetres that could be allocated to each person, if all the world's population were on the Isle of Wight. Which means that it is still possible for everyone in the world to stand up, but not lie down simultaneously, on the Isle of Wight. Though the travel arrangements in getting them there could well prove to be insuperable.

685

*'Yet, who can help loving the land that has taught us
Six hundred and eighty-five ways to dress eggs?'*
Thomas Moore, 1779-1852

687

earth days in a year on Mars.

688

The number of Friday the Thirteenths every 400 years. Because the Gregorian calendar (→365) provides 146,097 days in its 400 year cycle, and 146,097 is divisible by 7, it means that one complete cycle will take exactly 20,871 weeks, and the next cycle will begin on the same day of the week. Since there are 4800 months in 400 years, each of which has one thirteenth day, and 4,800 is not divisible by 7, there must be an imbalance in the distribution of those thirteenth days among the seven days of the week. In fact, there are 685 Monday the Thirteenths, 685 Tuesday the Thirteenths, 687 on Wednesday, 684 on Thursday, 688 on Friday, 684 on Saturday and 687 on Sunday. So the thirteenth of the month is more likely to fall on a Friday than any other day of the week.

696

bastards born in Rochdale, Lancashire, 1581-1640

710

pounds record weight of a pumpkin

711

Film: *711 Ocean Drive* (1950): Edmund O'Brien as a phone-tapper

725

homicides in England and Wales in 1991

732

survivors when the *Titanic* sank

736

convicts aboard the first British convict ship to land in Australia in 1788

737

number of a Boeing jet
cows in Pennard, Glastonbury, Somerset, milked to make 9 ft cheese for
    Queen Victoria in 1841

741

weeks in the US charts for Pink Floyd's 'Dark Side of the Moon'

750

herrings in a cran (approximately). A cran is the unit of volume for fresh-caught herrings. It is believed to be derived from a Scottish Gaelic word meaning 'portion' or 'allocation'. Under the Cran Measures Act of 1908, fresh herring had to be sold by the cran in certain places in the UK.

756

grams of bread eaten by the average Briton each week

759

miles travelled each year by the average Briton going shopping

763

people mentioned in the closing credits of 'Who Framed Roger Rabbit?' – but not Kathleen Turner, who was the voice of Jessica Rabbit.

777

'. . . the slightest consideration will show that though seven hundred and seventy-seven is a pretty large number, yet when you come to make a teenth of it, you will then see, I say, that the seven hundred and seventy-seventh part of a farthing is a good deal less than seven hundred and seventy-seven gold doubloons.'
Herman Melville, *Moby Dick*, 1851

777 is also the number of years to which the Old Testament prophet Lamech lived.

780

number of ostriches in Australia in 1922 according to government statistics

800

minimum weight of men's javelin in grams
warriors in Valhalla

Films include:
800 Leagues Down the Amazon (1993): adaptation of a Jules Verne
   adventure
800 Leagues Over the Amazon (1960): another Jules Verne adaptation
800 Two Lap Runners (1994): Japanese drama of athletics and love

803

grams of potatoes eaten by the average Briton each week

812

three-letter words in English

815

televisions per 1,000 people in the US in 1992

828

murders in Los Angeles in 1995

830

millimetres of rainfall in England and Wales in 1995

840

pedestrians run down and killed in Bogota, January 1995 to June 1996;
   drunken walking was made an offence in November 1996.

850

fixed stars catalogued by Hipparchus in 129 BC
number of words in the Basic English proposed by Professor C. K.
   Ogden in 1930

851

fifteen-letter words in English

854

bottles of Madeira William Pitt the Younger is said to have drunk in a single year (→2,410)

855

special terms and euphemisms used by the Stasi secret police in East Germany

870

length in feet of the side of a cube big enough to hold all the human blood in the world (according to John Allen Paulos)

871

catches taken by W. G. Grace

888

children reputedly fathered by Moulay Ismail (d. 1727), emperor of Morocco

911

the number to dial for emergencies in the US

915

aircraft lost by the RAF in the Battle of Britain

928

fishmongers' shops in Great Britain

930

years to which Adam lived according to the Old Testament

---

169 miles of railroad in Luxembourg

931

people personally killed by Behram, leader of the Thugee cult in India 1790-1830

946

company directors banned from running limited companies in the UK in 1996

950

years to which Noah lived in the Old Testament

962

years to which Jared lived in the Old Testament

963

length in feet of the *QE2*

969

years to which Methuselah lived – the greatest age of anyone mentioned in the Bible

976

the dialling code for the underworld in the following two films:
976-Evil (1988): shy teenager contacts Satan on the telephone
976-Evil 2: The Astral Factor (1991): Satan calls back

978

days of the longest recorded attack of sneezing

981

women killed in road accidents in the UK in 1994 (→2,251)

■ **989**

Film: *984: Prisoner of the Future* (1984): post-nuclear-holocaust prison
    drama

■ **989**

accidents on British railways in the year 1995-96

■ **1,000**

words a picture is worth
ships launched by face of Helen of Troy

Some currencies have 1,000 small units in a large unit:

There are 1,000	in a	in
millimes	dinar	Tunisia
millièmes	pound	Sudan
baiza	rial saidi	Oman
dirhams	dinar	Libya
fils	dinar	Jordan, Iraq, Bahrain
escudos	peso	Chile

1,000 is also popular in the cinema:
The House of a Thousand Candles (1936): from the spy story by Meredith
    Nicholson
Night Has a Thousand Eyes (1948): Edward G. Robinson in a tale of
    suspense
I Died a Thousand Times (1955): Jack Palance as a gangster with a heart
    of gold
Man of a Thousand Faces (1957): film biography of Lon Chaney Jr, with
    James Cagney
These Thousand Hills (1959): western based on the novel by
    A. B. Guthrie, Jr
The Thousand Eyes of Dr Mabuse (1960): Fritz Lang horror
A Thousand Clowns (1965): comedy that won a Best Supporting Actor
    Oscar for Martin Balsam
Night of a Thousand Cats (1972): madman breeds flesh-eating cats
1,000 Roses (1994): a Dutch allegory with a town overrun by roses and
    the hero going mad

1,001

Arabian nights
name of a British carpet cleaning fluid, with the pre-decimal currency
advertising slogan: 'One Thousand and One cleans a big, big carpet
for less than half-a-crown,'

Film: *A Thousand and One Nights* (1945): Cornel Wilde as Aladdin

1,003

women in Spain seduced by Mozart's Don Giovanni

1,016

recorded injuries in UK in 1993 involving baths

1,032

kilometres in the average length of a flight on a UK airline (→317)

1,046

winter population of Antarctica

1,071

Film:
1,071 Fifth Ave. (1994): documentary on the life of Frank Lloyd Wright

1,074

dollars per capita spent each year on defence in the US (→583)

1,082

establishments in Bangkok in January 1995 offering sexual services

1,092

television broadcast stations in the US

1,093

patents in the name of Thomas Edison

Edison and his phonograph |1878|

1,114

most votes polled by Screaming Lord Sutch (of the Monster Raving Loony Party) in a British by-election (Rotherham 1994)

■ 1,146

radios per 1,000 people in the UK in 1992

1,163

weight in tons of the statue of Christ in Rio de Janeiro

1,173

prisoners taken by Cuba at the disastrous Bay of Pigs invasion in 1961

1,177

centimetres in the average annual rainfall at Tutunendo, Colombia, another claimant (→468) for the title of the wettest place on earth

1,182

murders in New York in 1995

1,189

chapters in the Bible
persons prosecuted between December 1719 and November 1720 for

'lewd and disorderly practices' by the Societies for Promoting a Reformation of Manners

1,190

patients vasectomised in one day in Bangkok in December 1983

1,196

islands in the Maldives (→203)
people killed on roads of Morocco in first six months of 1996

1,198

killed when the *Lusitania* was torpedoed in 1915

1,225

miles a year travelled by the average Briton commuting to work

1,253

airports in Argentina

1,257

female deaths from suicide and undetermined injury in UK in 1996

1,300

average capacity of a female European brain in cubic centimetres

1,303

accidents in UK homes in 1994 involving slippers

1,350

population of Belgrade in 1733

1,440

minutes in a day

1,422

lines in the role of Hamlet

1,450

average capacity of male European brain in cubic centimetres

1,455

vasectomies performed in Iran, March to September 1996

1,482

feet height of Petronas Towers, Kuala Lumpur, the world's tallest
habitable building

1,486

bastards born in Rochdale, Lancashire, 1781-1820

1,493

passengers lost, excluding crew (out of 2,200), on the *Titanic* in 1912

1,513

passengers and crew killed when the *Titanic* sank in 1912
people rescued by the RAF in 1996

1,523

tradesmen in England and Wales prosecuted for opening on a Sunday
1708-09

1,586

daily papers in the US

1,590

pounds of domestic waste per capita in the US each year

1,594

fourteen-letter words in English

1,600

references in the Bible hostile to left-handers

1,632

miles walked each year by the average US policeman

1,638

lectures at first World Congress of Psychotherapy in Vienna in 1996

1,652

languages and dialects spoken in India

1,658

metres span of the Forth Rail Bridge

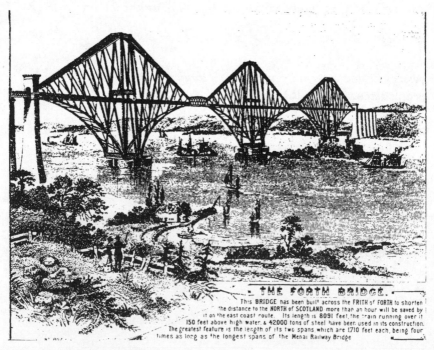

THE FORTH BRIDGE.

This BRIDGE has been built across the FRITH of FORTH to shorten the distance to the NORTH of SCOTLAND more than an hour will be saved by it on the east coast route. Its length is 8091 feet, the train running over it 150 feet above high water, & 42000 tons of steel have been used in its construction. The greatest feature is the length of its two spans which are 1710 feet each, being four times as long as the longest spans of the Menai Railway Bridge

1,686

television sets per square kilometre in Singapore

1,710

Test match runs scored by Viv Richards in 1976

1,728

in a great gross
cubic inches in a cubic foot
words in the biggest vocabulary of a budgerigar

1,729

This number features in one of the best-loved mathematical anecdotes. The story goes that the great Indian mathematician Ramanujan was being visited in hospital by his friend, mentor and fellow genius, G. H. Hardy. On arriving, Hardy mentioned that he had hoped to be able to make an interesting comment about the number of the taxi he came in, but it was a very uninteresting number, 1,729. 'Oh Hardy, Oh Hardy,' Ramanujan is said to have retorted instantly, going on to point out that 1,729 is the smallest number that can be expressed as the sum of the cubes of two positive numbers in two distinct ways: $1,729 = 12^3+1^3 = 10^3+9^3$. The most difficult thing to believe about this tale is that Hardy had not also realised it immediately – unless he was just keeping quiet about it in order to cheer up his sick friend.

1,733

aircraft lost by the Luftwaffe in the Battle of Britain

1,747

guns seized by police in Japan in 1994

1,750

new pet products launched in the US 1980-92

1,752

canons in the Code of Canon Law

1,757

cinema screens in Great Britain

1,766

hours of sunshine in England and Wales in 1995
miles length of Danube, Europe's longest river

1,770

There is a beach resort called 'Seventeen Seventy' in Bustard Bay,
  Queensland, named after the year James Cook landed there.
1,770 is also the number of words in common English on which there is
  no general agreement on the preferred spelling (according to Lee
  Deighton in 1972).

1,821

height in feet of CN Tower in Toronto, the world's tallest man-made
  self-supporting structure

1,837

Film: *1837* (1951): love story set at the time of the Canadian rebellion
  against England

1,855

times the word 'Lord' is in the Bible

1,860

Film: *1860* (1933): a priest, a shepherd and an intellectual caught up in
  Sicilian revolt

1,888

year requiring most Roman numerals: MDCCCLXXXVIII

■ **1,897**

miles covered by the Shah of Iran's Lamborghini Miura SVJ in 25 years

1,900

Film: *1900* (1976): Burt Lancaster, Donald Sutherland and Robert de Niro in twentieth-century Italian history

1,909

letters in the full chemical name for tryptophan synthetase

1,918

Film: *1918* (1985): small Texas town comes to terms with World War I

1,919

Film: *1919* (1983): old lady reminisces about Sigmund Freud

1,931

Film: *1931: Once Upon a Time in New York* (1972): bootlegging drama

1,941

Film: *1941* (1979): Stephen Spielberg flop with Dan Aykroyd and John Belushi in slapstick World War II film

1,969

Film: *1969* (1989): effect of Vietnam on US teenagers politico-comedy drama

1,984

Title of a novel by George Orwell, filmed as:
1984 (1956): Edmund O'Brien is Winston Smith – withdrawn from circulation after legal problems with George Orwell's estate
1984 (1984): John Hurt as Winston Smith; Richard Burton also stars in his last film

1,985

title of a novel (in homage to Orwell) by Anthony Burgess

1,993

deaths by scorpion sting in Mexico in 1946

1,994

men shaved in 60 minutes by Denny Rowe in Herne Bay in 1988

2,000

A popular film number:
2,000 Maniacs (1964): Civil War ghost horror
2,000 Weeks (1970): wife finds out about husband's mistress, Australian
   drama
2,000 Women (1944): Dame Flora Robson in prison drama
2,000 Year Old Man (1982): cartoon of Mel Brooks and Carl Reiner
   sketches
2,000 Years Later (1969): Roman soldier awakes in modern times

2,001

Film: *2001: A Space Odyssey* (1968): Kubrick's sci-fi classic, which won
   an Oscar for Special Effects

2,010

Film: *2010: The Year We Make Contact* (1984): the sequel to '2001'

2,020

Film: *2020 Texas Gladiators* (1985): post-apocalyptic action

2,118

radios per thousand people in the US in 1992

2,159

miles diameter of the moon

2,240

pounds in a ton

2,251

men killed in car crashes in the UK in 1994 (→981)

2,300

Americans declared missing in action in the Vietnam war

2,311

poetry books published in the UK in 1996

2,343

exclamation marks in Tom Wolfe's 'Bonfire of the Vanities'

2,362

feet length of the platform at Bournemouth railway station, the longest in the UK

2,381

bastards born in Rochdale, Lancashire, 1721-1820

2,396

marriages in Sweden in 1990 between male doctors and female nurses (→31)

2,410

bottles of port William Pitt the Younger is said to have drunk in a single year

2,473

sheets of paper used by Mrs Marva Drew in typing out every number from one to a million

2,555

times a year an average British man fantasises about having sex

2,589

British casualties in air raids in World War I

2,639

manatees in Florida in 1996 – the most ever

2,780

record number of baked beans eaten in 30 minutes, one by one with a cocktail stick

2,826

four-letter words in English

2,876

wickets taken by W. G. Grace

2,895

thirteen-letter words in English

2,983

sufferers from scofula touched by Charles II in 1669

3,000

Film: *The 3,000-Mile Chase* (1977): drugs and gangsters

3,103

prostitutes examined by the Metropolitan Police in 1837

3,106

carats of the Cullinan diamond

3,189

kilometres of motorway in Great Britain

3,203

deaths from motor vehicle accidents in England and Wales in 1995

3,212

feet drop of the Angel waterfall, Venezuela

3,274

miles diameter of Ganymede, moon of Jupiter, the largest moon in the solar system

3,398

people killed on Britain's roads in 1996

3,407

feet average depth of the Arctic Ocean

3,458

deaths from traffic accidents in the UK in 1994

3,516

phone calls made or received per year in the average US household

3,547

deaths from suicide in England and Wales in 1995

3,590

total staff at the 1997 Wimbledon Lawn Tennis Championships

3,658

men serving jail sentences in England and Wales for sexual offences

183 parishes in Iceland

■ **3,708**

to 1, odds against a professional golfer making a hole-in-one on a
   particular hole

■ **3,712**

murders in California in 1994

■ **3,717**

candidates in the British General Election of 1997

■ **3,793**

members of the American Ostrich Association in June 1995

184 square kilometres of Belgrade

- **3,808**

people injured in bed in the UK in 1993

- **3,887**

male deaths from suicide and undetermined injury in UK in 1996

- **3,901**

lines in Hamlet

- **3,994**

oak trees used to build Windsor Castle in the fourteenth century

4,045

rapes in England and Wales in 1991

4,065

capacity of Metropolitan Opera, New York

4,077

Mobile Army Service Hospital in M*A*S*H

4,115

summer population of Antarctica

4,145

length of the River Nile in miles

4,150

average annual car mileage in the UK

4,184

joules in a calorie

4,224

Bishops in the world according to the Vatican, February 1997

4,280

buffaloes killed by Buffalo Bill

4,613

twelve-letter words in English

4,616

feet of the Humber Bridge, the world's longest suspension bridge

---

4,824

most footnotes in an article in the *Law Review*

4,830

British casualties in air raids in World War I

4,840

square yards in an acre

4,870

horse race wins by Sir Gordon Richards

4,907

five-letter words in English

4,968

people in the world for every doctor

5,000

Films include:
The 5,000 Fingers of Dr T (1953): musical fantasy with 500 child slaves
    forced to play the piano
Five Thousand Dollars on One Ace (1964): gambling and death

5,040

changes in a bellringer's classic eight-bell peal of 'doubles'
ideal number of households in a city state according to Plato's Laws

5,123

kilowatt hours of electricity consumed per capita in the UK each year

5,267

men serving jail sentences in England and Wales for robbery

5,280

feet in a mile

5,435

miles of the balloon flight made by Steve Fossett in 1995 from South Korea to Canada. He broke this record in 1997 when failing in an attempt to go round the world in a balloon.

5,444

members of Skoptzy sect – who believed in self castration – on Russian police records in 1875

5,544

area of Connecticut in square miles

5,624

water mills recorded in the Domesday book

5,630

umbrellas left on LMS Railway in 1946

5,683

new beverage brands launched in the US 1980-92

5,748

'It is two good miles, and just five thousand, seven hundred and forty-eight steps.'
Jonathan Swift, *Journal to Stella,* 1711

5,938

men serving sentences in jails in England and Wales for burglary

6,000

Film: *6,000 Enemies* (1939): Walter Pigeon is the DA framed by the mob

6,137

performances of *A Chorus Line* on Broadway

6,250

people per public lavatory in Guangzhou, China

6,511

miles travelled within Britain each year by the average Briton

6,563

establishments in Thailand in January 1995 offering sexual services

6,704

eleven-letter words in English

6,949

patent number of Abraham Lincoln's sole invention: 'A Device for Buoying Vessels over Shoals'

7,000

number of people meditating simultaneously that it takes to influence world affairs according to Maharishi Mahesh Yogi

7,254

Film: *7254* (1971): war drama

7,612

parking tickets issued to the Soviet UN mission in 1989

7,910

six-letter words in English

7,985

road fatalities in the UK in 1966, the worst year on record

8,280

miles from Chicago to Hong Kong on the world's longest nonstop air trip, with United Airlines, inaugurated in July 1996

8,515

men serving jail sentences in England and Wales for violence against the person

8,771

women arrested for prostitution in England and Wales in the year to 29 September 1857

8,833

horse race winners ridden by Willie Shoemaker

9,000

the weight in grammes of 9,000 metres of yarn is equal to its number of denier

9,091

people per doctor in Swaziland – the world's worst ratio

9,153

ten-letter words in English

9,353

entries in the first Chinese dictionary, compiled in AD 100

9,665

shoe shops in Great Britain

9,906

seven-letter words in English

10,000

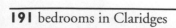

Films:
Ten Thousand Bedrooms (1957): musical comedy with Dean Martin
10,000 Dollars Blood Money (1966): Italian film about a bounty hunter

10,404

dispensing chemists in Great Britain

10,442

different words in the King James Bible, according to Lincoln Bennett

10,791

nine-letter words in English

11,033

eight-letter words in English

11,174

Test runs scored by Allan Border

11,610

words in the role of Hamlet

11,738

camels in Australia in 1922

12,139

Americans who bet on General Noriega's prison number in the first
Florida State Lottery after his arrest

12,634

butchers' shops in Great Britain

12,769

people killed by handguns in the US in 1994

13,240

penises cut off as trophies of the ancient Egyptian victory of Pharaoh
Meneptah over the Libyans at Karnak

13,272

sex workers in Bangkok

13,387

airports in the US

13,759

miles along the frontier of China

14,299

pounds of jellies, pickles and hams sold at the Great Exhibition of 1851

15,487

pages in the first completed revised edition of the *Oxford English Dictionary*

15,502

people per square mile in San Francisco

15,771

height of Mont Blanc in feet

16,091

deaths from injury and poisoning in the UK in 1996

16,136

gun murders in the US in 1993

17,561

kilometres of railway in the UK

17,677

different words used by Shakespeare

17,968

kilometres of the coastline of Antarctica

18,033

traffic accidents on the roads of Morocco in the first six months of 1996

20,000

A popular number in films:
20,000 Leagues Under the Sea (1916): silent classic
20,000 Years in Sing-Sing (1933): Spencer Tracy as a reformed criminal in love with Bette Davis

---

193 centimetres of snow in a day

20,000 Men a Year (1939): adventure thriller with Randolph Scott
20,000 Leagues Under the Sea (1954): Kirk Douglas and James Mason in
   Disney's version of Jules Verne, which won an Oscar for Special
   Effects
20,000 Eyes (1961): embezzler steals from gangster suspense
The 20,000-Pound Kiss (1963): Edgar Wallace mystery with Dawn
   Addams

■ **20,352**

people killed by scorpions in Mexico 1940-49

■ **21,785**

words in the *OED* that had their first appearance in the eighteenth
century

■ **23,305**

murders in the US in 1994

■ **23,530**

gallstones removed from an eighty-five-year-old woman in Worthing,
   Sussex in 1987

■ **25,550**

bottles of suntan lotion bought by the US Army from one K-Mart store
   in Georgia in the month after Iraq invaded Kuwait

26,963

kilograms of milk in 377 days mostly in 1995 produced by Acme Gold 2nd at Kettering, Northants – a new world record for one (slightly extended) year's production

27,457

times Shakespeare used the word 'the'

29,022

height of Everest in feet

29,899

words used by James Joyce in *Ulysses*

30,107

clothes stores in Great Britain

30,135

police officers in New York city

30,510

square kilometres in Belgium

31,388

parking violation tickets ignored by the Russian UN mission in New York in 1996

32,354

words listed in the *OED* that were already in the language by 1400

32,429

labrador retrievers registered by the Kennel Club – making it the UK's most popular pedigree breed

---

195 countries where Coca-Cola is sold

32,738

homicides in Colombia in 1996

35,797

feet depth of Marianas trench in Pacific – the deepest spot in the ocean

35,810

words in the *OED* that had their first appearance in the 16th century

40,000

Film: *Forty Thousand Horsemen* (1941): war story with Chips Rafferty

41,522

traffic accidents on roads in Morocco in 1995 – the country with the world's worst accident rate per car

41,530

Sherman tanks produced in World War II

42,551

bombs dropped on Japan in July 1945

43,560

square feet in one acre

44,473

seriously injured on Britain's roads in 1996

46,227

times the word 'and' appears in the Bible

46,773

words in the *OED* that had their first appearance in the seventeenth century

50,000

Just two films to note:
50,000 BC (Before Clothing) (1963): sex comedy
Fifty Thousand Dollar Reward (1924): silent western

51,047

average daily prison population in England and Wales in 1995

52,415

people per square mile in Manhattan

52,481

words in this book including the bibliography, footnotes and index

54,393

people in British jails in May 1996

54,589

deaths on the road in the US in 1972, the record number for a calendar year

■ **54,659**

Americans injured by ovens and stoves in 1991

54,896

runs made by W. G. Grace

59,328

motorcycles sold in the UK in 1996

■ **60,559**

words in the *OED* that had their first appearance in the nineteenth century

■ **63,360**

inches in a mile

■ **64,747**

dollars in each US family's share of the national debt

■ **68,578**

deaths in London caused by the great plague of 1664-5 according to official figures

■ **70,000**

Film: *70,000 Witnesses* (1932): someone is murdered at a football game

■ **71,280**

prostitutes in Indonesia in 1994, according to official figures

■ **71,852**

possible positions in a chess game after Black's second move

■ **73,884**

people killed by the atom bomb dropped on Nagasaki, 9 August 1945

■ **75,981**

the chance of being murdered within the next year for a UK resident is 1 in 75,981

■ **80,000**

Film: *80,000 Suspects* (1963): Claire Bloom in a tale of smallpox in Bath

■ **86,400**

seconds in a day

■ **88,888**

account number for Nick Leeson's illicit Barings operations in Singapore

100,000

when the Ukraine changed its currency from the karbovanets to the hryvnia in 1996, the exchange rate was 100,000 karbovantsi to 1 hryvnia

101,504

books published in the UK in 1996

101,683

convictions secured by the Societies for Promoting a Reformation of Manners for offences against public decency between 1698 and 1738

106,307

seminarians studying philosophy and theology, according to Vatican in February 1997

131,153

complaints to local authorities in the UK about noisy neighbours in 1993-94

134,281

parking tickets ignored by UN diplomats in New York in 1996

142,807

people killed in the Tokyo-Yokohama earthquake in 1923

144,000

days in a 'baktun' – 400 years of the Mayan calendar, each year comprising 18 weeks each of 20 days

149,547

spectators at the Scotland-England football match at Hampden Park in 1937

151,485

miles length of the coastline of Canada

---

200 pounds for passing Go in Monopoly

155,499

divorces in England and Wales in 1995

174,465

patent number for Bell's telephone, the most valuable patent

177,737

most pogo stick jumps

186,272

speed of light in miles per sec

187,880

lakes in Finland

211,208

square miles of France

223,898

US patent number for Edison's electric light

289,996

shops in Great Britain according to the latest (1997) statistics

308,982

male deaths in the UK in 1995

324,198

stars catalogued by Friedrich Argelander in his *Bonner Durchmusterung*,
1859-62

331,248

marriages in the UK in 1994

---

201 heliports in South Korea

332,730

female deaths in the UK in 1995

366,999

kilometres of public roads in Great Britain

398,671

British troops killed in the first battle of the Somme in 1916

404,750

priests on earth according to the Vatican in February 1997

414,825

entries in the *OED* (first complete revised edition, 1933)

450,000

cubic cubits volume of Noah's Arc (300 cubits long by 50 wide and 30 high)

529,000

Film: *The $529,000 Boo-Boo* (1971): a hermit is accidentally credited with a large sum of money by his bank

565,939

pills taken by C. H. A. Kilner of Zimbabwe between 1967 and 1988

640,145

number of the US population who were born in England (1990 census)

658,958

flights made by UK airlines in 1995

773,696

words in the King James Bible

802,701

Final year arrived at by the traveller in H. G. Wells' *The Time Machine*

870,027

plain buns sold at the Great Exhibition of 1851

934,691

Bath buns sold at the Great Exhibition of 1851

967,500

square miles area of Sudan (the largest country in Africa)

1,000,000

When the word 'million' occurs in a film title, there is a greater than one-in-three chance that the next word will be 'dollar'.

Here are some 'million' films:
If I Had a Million (1932): George Raft and W. C. Fields in a crime comedy
Million Dollar Legs (1932): comedy with Ben Turpin and W. C. Fields
Million Dollar Ransom (1934): based on a story by Damon Runyon *One Million Dollars Ransom*
I Stole a Million (1939): George Raft and Jason Robards in crime mystery
Tanks a Million (1941): war comedy
Million-Dollar Baby (1941): comedy drama with Ronald Reagan
The Missing Million (1942): based on a book by Edgar Wallace
A Girl in a Million (1946): Michael Hordern and Joan Greenwood in a comedy
Million-Dollar Mermaid (1952): Walter Pigeon and Victor Mature in a swimming spectacular
The Beast With a Million Eyes (1956): sci-fi horror western
Million-Dollar Collar (1964): a tale of a performing dog and jewel smugglers

How to Steal a Million (1966): Audrey Hepburn hires Peter O'Toole to do a robbery

One Million Years BC (1967): prehistoric anachronisms with Raquel Welch

The Million Eyes of Su-Muru (1967): spy story with Klaus Kinski and Shirley Eaton

Million-Dollar Duck (1971): Disney fantasy with golden eggs

A Million to Juan (1994): based on Mark Twain's story: *The Million-Dollar Banknote*

1,226,467

people saw the Tutankhamum exhibition at Metropolitan Museum in New York 1978-79

1,238,085

pounds taken on the opening day of *Batman Forever* in the UK

1,694,117

attendance at the Tutankhamum exhibition at the British Museum 1972-73

2,000,000

A good number for eccentric films:

The Two Million Clams of Cap'n Jack (1973): George Peppard drama

Cop Gives Waitress $2 Million Tip (1994): romantic comedy with Bridget Fonda

2,054,754

pounds of the largest unclaimed prize in the British National Lottery

2,367,234

Malaysian 20-sen coins used to set a world record in 1996 for the longest line of coins. The mark to beat is now 55.63 kilometres.

3,586,489

letters in the Bible

4,000,000

The Four Million, a short story by O. Henry

5,000,000

Film: *Five Million Years to Earth* (1968): sci-fi horror

5,118,470

pairs of green socks bought for US armed forces in 1989

5,195,930

Britons who emigrated to the US between 1820 and 1994

5,506,720

documents classified as secret or top secret by the US government in 1989

6,000,000

Film: *Cyborg: The Six-Million Dollar Man* (1973): with Lee Majors

6,469,952

spots drawn by animators for the Disney film of *101 Dalmatians*

7,126,132

Germans who emigrated to the US between 1820 and 1994

8,000,000

Film: *8 Million Ways to Die* (1985): Jeff Bridges in a cops, pimps and prostitutes drama

8,765,832

hours from the start of 1 January 2,000 until the end of 31 December 2,999

---

205 square kilometres in Cincinnati

10,000,000

ergs in a joule
Film: *The Ten Million Dollar Getaway* (1991): made-for-TV drama of a
1978 robbery at Kennedy Airport

11,914,200

new car registrations in Western Europe in 1994

13,247,091

square miles in the British Commonwealth at the beginning of 1997

20,000,000

Films:
20 Million Miles to Earth (1957): US rocket to Venus brings back
rampaging alien
20 Million Sweethearts (1934): Ginger Rogers and Dick Powell in a
musical comedy

50,000,000

Film: *Fifty Million Frenchmen* (1931): Cole Porter musical comedy

53,310,761

Elvis Presley's army serial number

58,489,975

population of the UK

107,689,927

animals killed by the US fur trade between 1919 and 1921

148,081,443

cars in the US (which works out at 1.8 persons per car)

266,476,278

population of the US in July 1996

■ 399,902,004

angels in the universe: in nine choirs of 6,666 legions, each legion having 6,666 spirits according to mediaeval theologians

■ 500,000,000

Film: *Objective 500 Million* (1966): French-Italian co-production on a plot to steal 500m Francs

■ 1,000,000,000

In the sixteenth century, the English invented the term 'billion' to mean a million million. All went well until the late eighteenth century when the French started using the word *'billion'* to mean a thousand million. The Americans then copied the French usage. For the first half of the twentieth century there was confusion between American and British billions, but since the 1950s, the British have increasingly followed the Franco-American lead. The correct prefix for a billion of anything is 'giga-'.

A billion, as seen in the films:
Billion Dollar Brain (1967): Ken Russell directs Michael Caine in the Len Deighton story
The Billion Dollar Hobo (1932): man has to live as tramp to collect inheritance
A Billion for Boris (1990): man rewires television to pick up programmes from the future
Mr Billion (1977): Jackie Gleason comedy adventure

■ 9,000,000,000

Short story: 'The Nine Billion Names of God' by Arthur C. Clark

■ 9,192,631,770

cycles of resonance vibration of the caesium-133 atom in a second. Since 1967 this has been the formal scientific definition of a second

■ 4,985,567,071,200

dollars of US national debt when the clock stopped near Times Square, New York, on 14 November 1995

Bibliography

Innumerable works of reference have been consulted in the compilation of this book. The following list includes some of the most useful and intriguing.

Works on Numbers:

The Guinness Book of Numbers (1989), Adrian Room – a useful general work on the history of numbers, with a good deal of quirky information

The Mystery of Numbers (1993), Annemarie Schimmel – all the mysticism and religious symbolism of numbers

The Penguin Dictionary of Curious and Interesting Numbers (1986), David Wells – everything you want to know about the mathematical side of numbers

General Reference Works on CD-Rom:

The Oxford English Dictionary – generally viewed as a collection of words, this fine work is also very rich in numbers

The Oxford Interactive Encyclopedia

The World Book Multimedia Encyclopedia

The Hutchinson Multimedia Encyclopedia

The New Grolier Multimedia Encyclopedia – the search facility on all these CD-Roms enables one to look up numbers in a way that was impossible with traditional alphabetical ordering

The Complete Works of Jane Austen – not renowned for her use of numbers, this authoress does, however, include some useful observations on 19, 48, 100, 130 and the size of dinner-parties

The Complete Works of William Shakespeare – a writer whose skill with words has been allowed unfairly to overshadow his general numeracy

The Bible – a rich source of numerical references, although its own 'Book of Numbers' is disappointing in this respect

Subsidiary sources:

Concise Oxford Dictionary of the Christian Church (1977), ed. Elizabeth Livingstone – contains a few useful numbers

All the Trouble in the World (1994), P. J. O'Rourke – full of useful statistics

The Black Arts (1967), Richard Cavendish – useful tips on numerology and alchemy

The Body (1985), Anthony Smith – contains many more numbers than the same author's *The Mind*

Brewer's Dictionary of Phrase and Fable (1894) – the first edition of this classic is by far the most numerate

Cluck! (1981), Jon-Stephen Fink – the definitive work on chickens in films

The Dent Dictionary of Measurement (1994), Mike Darton and John Clark – very useful

Human Development Report (1966), United Nations Development Programme – packed with useful figures

Innumeracy (1989), John Allen Paulos – with fewer numbers than one might expect, but those that appear are generally well chosen

The Larousse Dictionary of Science and Technology (1955) – more words than numbers, but still informative

Made in America (1994), Bill Bryson – a brilliantly informative collection of words and numbers

The Medieval Machine (1988), Jean Gimpel – a remarkable source of ancient numbers

The Mother Tongue, Bill Bryson – a prefect balance between numerical and verbal information

The New Penguin Dictionary of Music (1986) – a handy guide apart from its inconsistency on the number of Hungarian Rhapsodies written by Liszt

Ostrich Egg-shell Cups of Mesopotamia and the Ostrich in Ancient and Modern Times (1926), Berthold Laufer – a classic

Phrenology (1969), Orson Squire Fowler and Lorenzo Niles Fowler – a modern reprint of a nineteenth century classic on head bumps

Population Trends (1996), Office for National Statistics – full of numbers, though rather too many are rounded to the nearest thousand

Sex in Georgian England (1994), A. D. Harvey – definitive

Sports Spectators (1986), Allen Gutman – an indispensable history of non-participation

The Total Package (1995), Thomas Hine – all you need to know about cans, boxes and tubes

The Top Ten of Everything (1997), Russell Ash – the thinking man's book of records

What Counts – The Complete Harper's Index (1991), ed: Charis Conn and Ilena Silverman – a fine collection of figures, sadly not arranged in numerical order

Index

Items or topics counted, measured or otherwise enumerated in the text (references are to the **numbers** under which relevant items appear)

boat races 1; 68; 73; 143
bobsleigh 145
Bolivia 94
bombs 58; 91; 144; 315;
    42,551; 73,884
bones 29; 30; 31; 32;
    205; 206
books 22; 83; 142; 143
boots 186
booze 50
bores 312
Borneo 177
bottle-banks 17
bottles 2; 4; 6; 8; 10; 12;
    16; 27; 140
bottoms 17
bowling 10; 15
boxes 42
boxing 19; 49; 52; 59;
    67; 91; 175; 181
brain 14; 162; 1,300;
    1,450
bread 756
breakfast 135
breasts 50
brides 7
bridge 12; 13; 30; 40;
    134; 1,658; 4,626
bronze 8
Brooklyn 181
brothels 85; 1,082;
    6,563
brothers 7
brussels sprout 18
Bucharest 203
buckets 57
Budapest 203
Buddha 45; 181; 394
budgerigar 1,728
buffaloes 50; 54; 4,280
buildings 43; 56; 102;
    1,482
bullets 22; 39
bullocks 67; 152
butlers 1
butter 36

caber 82
Cairo 215
cakes 36; 85; 870,027;
    934,691

calendar 11; 31; 52; 60;
    260; 365; 688;
    144,000
camels 23; 50; 57; 62;
    315; 11,738
Canada 3; 54; 87; 155;
    282; 151,385
canals 169; 171
cannonballs 56
canons 203; 1,752
capital punishment 92;
    222
caravans 618
carbon 28
cardinals 120
carrots 50; 360
Carussi, Jacopo da 5
castration 5; 5,444
Catch 22
cathedrals 43; 145; 157;
    158; 170; 365; 366;
    466; 555; 579
cats 5; 9; 34; 38; 50;
    420
cemeteries 450
censorship 231
centipedes 46; 175
chains 80
Channel Tunnel 13; 31
chapters 22; 66; 114;
    1,189
characters 6
Charles, Prince 2
checkouts 15
cheese 9; 19; 22; 30; 50;
    108; 115; 370
chemists 10,404
Chernobyl 31
chess 13; 17; 64
chewing 32
chicken 78; 102; 227
children 17; 22; 31; 50;
    63; 888
China 14; 16; 21; 25;
    37; 41; 50; 80; 121;
    6,250; 13,759
chocolate 5; 8
Christmas 3; 4; 12; 37;
    38; 155; 364
chromosomes 10; 16;
    22; 26; 38; 46; 48; 78

cigarettes 97; 114
Cincinnati 205
cinemas 483; 1,757
circumcision 8; 99
cities 23; 58; 83; 280
civet 28
civil servants 50
clock 13
cloth 114
clothes 35; 50; 54;
    30,107
coastlines 124; 148;
    161; 151,485
Coca-Cola 13; 114;
    195;. 210; 343
cocaine 50
cockroach 16
coconut 9; 50
coffee 11; 12; 25; 50
coins 2,367,234
Colombia 32,738
colonies 13
colonists 117
colours 3; 4
columns 104
comets 37; 76
commandments 10; 279
Commonwealth 53;
    13,247,091
communists 151
compact disc 74
complaints 131,153
computers 18; 170
condoms 50; 52
condors 89
confectionery 50
Connecticut 5,444
consent, age of 10
consonants 22; 34
constellations 48; 88
constipation 102
contact lenses 50
conversations 96
convicts 50; 57; 108;
    206; 279; 290; 736;
    3,658; 5,267; 5,938;
    8,515; 51,047;
    54,393
copper 9
coral 35
corners of the earth 4

films 85; 194; 246; 763
fingers 4; 5; 8; 10; 16;
    5,000
Finland 15; 187,880
Fire of London 6
fish 48; 50; 115; 143;
    153
fjords 204
flags 13
floods 17; 40; 112; 122
flour 57
flowers 4
football 11; 18; 27; 66;
    90; 100; 105; 106;
    119; 149,547
footnotes 4,824
forest 50
fox 42; 51
France 4; 22; 38; 72; 96;
    140; 370; 466;
    211,208
Freedoms 4
French hens 3
frogs 4; 26
fruit 4
fucks 38
Furies 3
furlongs 8; 220

gables 7
gallons 4; 126; 288
gallstones 23,530
games 177
garbage 23; 1,590
garlic 10
gates 63
geese a-laying 6
Gemini presidents 1
Germans 7,126,132
gestation 16; 19; 22; 31;
    40; 42; 50; 51; 113;
    150; 175; 266; 315;
    336; 352; 365; 660
gill 5
gloves 50
goals 30
goats 19; 50; 138; 150
gods 9; 99
gogo bars 78
gold 22; 24; 49; 50
gold rings 5; 17

golden vampires 7
goldfish 17; 41
golf 1; 2; 3; 4; 14; 18;
    46; 72; 267; 270;
    3,708
gonorrhoea 17
Graces 3
grains 24; 218
gramophone records 33;
    45; 78
grapefruit 44; 50
grapes 16
graves 5
greenfly 10
Gross National Product
    80
Guam 208
guns 19; 21; 38; 39; 44;
    45; 47; 63; 91; 1,747;
    12,769; 16,136

Hades 5; 19
hailstones 92; 246
haircuts 18; 160
hairs 1; 52; 56; 65
Haiti 1; 370
hamsters 11; 16; 22
handkerchiefs 39
hands 4; 16; 55
hardness 10
harpsichord 70
hats 6; 57
heads of state 110
heart 48; 72; 140; 201
heavens 7; 50
hedgehogs 34; 35; 250
height 46; 50; 55; 64;
    65; 70; 76; 96; 157;
    193
helicopters 61; 75
hell 9
hexominoes 35
hibernation 50
hiccup 1; 68
hills 7
hockey 6; 11; 25; 39
hoes 3
holes 18; 72; 91; 146
holidays 159
Holy Grail 42
homosexuals 234

honey 45
hops 50
horns 8
horse-races 11; 30; 121;
    147; 4,870; 8,833
horses 18; 52; 62; 164;
    173; 205; 336; 340
hotel rooms 53; 191
hours 24
housebreaking 68
households 5,040
houses, astrological 12
housework 62
human being 46; 266
human rights 44; 93
humours 4
hurdles 33; 36; 39; 84;
    122
hurricanes 11; 137; 184
hydrogen 15

ice 12
ice cream 99
Iceland 5; 183
idiots 159; 208
Immortals 40
inches 12; 18; 36
India 54; 58; 179; 202;
    468; 1,652
Indians, Little 10
infidelity 50
intestines 29
inventions 533; 1,093;
    6,949; 174,465;
    233,898
Ireland 26
iron 4
ISBN 11
islands 12; 18; 33; 59;
    73; 97; 106; 132;
    149; 155; 187; 195;
    203; 204; 1,196
isotope 210; 235
Israel 12; 40; 42; 120;
    273
Italians 17
ivory 14

Jamaica 82
javelin 29; 600; 800
jellybeans 12

jewellery 16
joules 4,184
journalists 56; 123
just men 4

kangaroo 64
keys 7; 24; 88
kidneys 190
kings 8; 18
kitchen scales 3
knee-tags 16
koala 8; 22
Kuwait 640; 25,550

labours 12
lace 13
ladies dancing 9
lakes 4; 12; 82; 143;
    145; 187,880
languages 14; 16; 21;
    22; 23; 25; 44; 47;
    50; 58; 149; 179;
    349; 1,652
larceny 177
lashes 39; 85
laughs 17
lavatories 24; 50; 398;
    666; 6,250
leather 2
lectures 1,638
legs 4; 5; 8; 46
letters 4; 5; 12; 21; 22;
    24; 26; 28; 29; 31;
    32; 45; 48; 72; 167;
    1,909; 3,586,489
Liberty, Statue of 47;
    189; 204
life expectancy 39; 70;
    79; 83
lifespan 123; 127; 175;
    365; 777; 930; 950;
    962; 969
lifts 64
lighthouses 82; 122; 208
lightning 81
ligulae 6
limbs 5
linen 12
lines 6
lions 103; 107; 176; 250
Lisbon 84

liver 55
livery 84
lives 9
llama 22; 340
lobsters 28
locks 7
lords 52
lords a-leaping 10
lotteries 13; 49; 50; 112;
    133; 12,139;
    2,054,754
lunatics 159
lynchings 130; 230; 577

magistrates 30
magnificent 7
maids a-milking 8
mail 50
Malawi 208
Maldives 203
mammals 16
manatees 2,639
Manchester 109
Mandela, Nelson 175
mangoes 50
Manhattan 24; 52,415
marches 75; 109; 136
margarine 41
marines 206
marlin 174
marriages 31; 37; 50;
    182; 2,396; 331,248
marrow 108
masses 93
meanings 22; 24; 194;
    214
measles 14
medals 15; 53; 178;
    182; 634
meditators 7,000
members of parliament
    21; 40; 47; 101; 120;
    155; 166; 179; 204;
    282; 659; 666
memory 7
menopause 7
menorah 7
mercury 32
meridiens 109
meteorites 118; 175
Methuselah 969

Mexico 31
mice 40
mice, blind 3
mice, laboratory 19
milk 19; 30; 97; 26,963
mingles 16
minks 50; 65
moles 25
monkeys 50; 56; 193
Monopoly 25; 28; 52;
    200
months 12; 28; 29; 30;
    31
moon 6; 12; 14; 28; 31;
    107; 111; 152; 173;
    2,159; 3,274
Mormons 31; 47; 148
Morocco 379; 888;
    1,196; 18,033;
    41,522
mosquito 587
Mother's day 50
motor-racing 31; 51
motorcycles 59,328
mountains 112; 15,771;
    29,022
moustache 63
mules 2; 37; 50
mummification 70
municipalities 169
murders 7; 16; 40; 55;
    57; 144; 171; 229;
    276; 677; 725; 828;
    931; 1,182; 3,712;
    16,136; 23,305;
    32,738; 75,981
muscles 17; 639
muses 9
music 22; 87; 116; 120;
    134; 175; 202; 240;
    303; 340; 440; 471;
    675; 741
musketeers 3
mutton 8

names 99;
    9,000,000,000
Napoleon 96; 157; 666
naucraries 48
nerves 43
netball 7; 11; 15

soldiers 80
soliciting 39; 103; 150
sonnets 154
sounds 47
soup 64
soya beans 52
space 75; 188; 203; 211
spaghetti 50
speed limit 25; 155
spellings 83; 127; 404;
1,770
Sphinx 185
sprinting 27
stamps 209; 325
Star Trek 79
starfish 5
stars 61; 171; 850;
324,198
states 11; 50
stations 42; 2,362
statues 167; 189; 204;
394; 563; 1,163
steel 11
steps 14; 39; 365; 577;
5,748
stitches 9; 16
stockings 110
stomach 32
stones 30; 180; 181;
189; 380
Stooges 3
storeys 56; 96; 110
strainers 5
stratagems 36
strawberries 23; 26
straws, drinking 11
streets 38
strikes 3
string quartets 24
strings 47
submarines 160
Sudan 967,500
sugar 136
suicides 341; 1,257;
3,547; 3,887
sun 109; 154; 155
sunglasses 50
suntan lotion 25,550
superstition 13; 17
swans a-swimming 7
sweat 4

Sweden 11; 31; 59; 115;
184; 2,396
sweets 5
Switzerland 91; 168;
183
syllables 14; 16; 17; 24;
31
symphonies 41; 66; 104

table napkins 26
tablets 12
tailors 9
Taj Mahal 187
tambourines 256
tangerines 23
tanks 41,530
tape measure 7
tarot 22
Tasmania 201
tea 28; 39
tea-cosies 0; 3
teacups 4
teeth 3; 7; 32; 42; 50;
98
telephones 1; 50; 224;
911; 976; 3,516;
174,465
telescope 94
televisions 23; 28; 50;
98; 435; 812
temperature 10; 31; 32;
34; 37; 51; 84; 91;
127; 136; 137; 138;
149; 183; 196; 212;
464
temples 47; 82; 89; 104
tennis 36; 64; 78; 156;
157; 167
tenses 23
terms of abuse 33
testicles 19
thermostat 4
theses 95
thieves 40
things 18
tidiness 50
tigers 190; 270
tiles 136
tin 10
tobacco 41
toes 4; 5; 6; 50; 185

tombs 62
tongues 45
tornadoes 148
Toronto 1,821
tourism 503
towns 23; 169; 192; 207
trades 43
traffic jam 84
traffic lights 6
trains 14; 29; 125; 166;
188; 231; 244; 989
tees 115; 130; 179; 329;
3,994
triangles 24; 45; 48; 60
tribes 12; 133; 155
tributaries 17
tricycle wheels 3
trombones 76
truck drivers 50
trumpets 7
Turkey 75; 90; 118; 198
turtle doves 2
type-faces 122
typing 5; 22
tyres 42

umbrellas 5,630
underground railways
19; 189; 249; 251;
266; 469
underpants 50
unicycles 1; 53
unions 158
United Nations 51; 181;
185
universities 37; 174

van Gogh 1; 5
variations 30; 33
varieties 57
vasectomies 435; 1,190;
1,499
Verona, Gentlemen of 2
verses 102; 107; 158;
286
vertebrae 26
video recorders 50
Vietnam 17; 2,300
violin concertos 16
virginity 50
virtues 3; 7